THE ECONOMIC THEORY OF THE WORKING CLASS

THE ECONOMIC THEORY OF THE WORKING CLASS

Geoffrey Kay
Lecturer in Economics
The City University, London

St. Martin's Press　　　　　　　　New York

© Geoffrey Kay 1979

All rights reserved. For information, write:
St. Martin's Press, Inc. 175 Fifth Avenue, New York, NY 10010
Printed in Great Britain
First published in the United States of America in 1979
ISBN 0-312-23668-9

Library of Congress Cataloging in Publication Data
Kay, G. B.
   The economic theory of the working class.

   Bibliography: p.
   Includes index.
   1. Labor economics. 2. Labor and laboring
classes. 3. Marxian economics. I. Title.
HD4901.K36   1979   335.4'12   78-23325
ISBN 0-312-23668-9

To I. I. Rubin and Bill Blake

Contents

Preface ix

1 ABSOLUTE POVERTY 1

2 THE ELEMENTS OF ECONOMIC THEORY 7
  1 Material production and basic reproduction 7
  2 Money 10
  3 Value and labour 20

3 SURPLUS VALUE 27
  1 From simple circulation to capital 27
  2 Surplus value 31
  3 Labour and labour-power 34
  4 The legitimacy of exploitation 39
  5 Formal definitions 42

4 ABSOLUTE AND RELATIVE SURPLUS VALUE 44
  1 Absolute surplus value 45
  2 Relative surplus value 48
  3 The modes combined 51

5 INDUSTRIAL CO-OPERATION AND MACHINE PRODUCTION 54
  1 Co-operation 55
  2 Machinery 63

6 WAGES 68
  1 The wage-form 68
  2 The 'immiseration' of labour 72
  3 Natural time and the turnover of capital 78
  4 The value of labour-power 85

7 PROFITS 92
1 The organic composition of capital 93
2 The concentration of capital 97
3 Social capital and the average rate of profit 104
4 Competition and the class struggle 112
5 Historical limits 116

8 THE RETURN OF THE RESERVE ARMY 120
1 Accumulation and unemployment 121
2 The 'double crisis' 124

NOTE: PRODUCTIVE AND UNPRODUCTIVE LABOUR 132

Suggested Reading 135

Index 136

Preface

The thesis of this short book is the complete and utter irrationality of capitalist production as a mode of satisfying human needs. Particular expressions of this are easily perceived: the ecology crisis and urban decay; the social conditions that turn new technologies which promise to lighten the burden of labour into threats of unemployment and poverty; the re-appearance of traditional forms of economic crises which see men and productive equipment idle despite the prevalence of scarcity and insecurity. But taken individually their significance as the symptoms of a world stood on its head is lost.

No attempt is made here to analyse any of these issues in detail. This is a work of theory which restricts itself to general conditions and is, therefore, abstract. But abstract in this sense does not mean unreal, artificial or academic, and I hope even the most impatient reader will appreciate the relevence of study at this level. There is, of course, always the danger of a theoretical work running away with itself and indulging in fine distinctions that have little or no meaning outside its covers. To the extent that this has been avoided, and the English language protected from many abuses heaped upon it in the first draft, thanks are due to Charmian Campbell who forcibly reminded me in any number of detailed ways of the futility of a generation of Marxists who, having discovered that Marx himself was readable, then made their own texts unintelligible. The immediate result was a chaotic manuscript to which Mary Keane brought order in the most difficult circumstances.

Another was the exclusion of all footnotes, which these days seem more like a cosmetic—or a disease—on the face of texts, rather than a useful tool of scholarship. This cleansing of the text was made much easier by an earlier decision to exclude all references to Marx, in order to avoid the danger of slipping from citing Marx as the source of an idea to citing him as proof of its correctness. The theory developed here is taken almost exclusively from Marx's writings, and the omission of his name is no attempt to disguise the nature of the work, which I hope will not be judged more or less 'Marxist' on this count alone. The title, which has the working class as both the subject and object of theory, is indicative of my intentions.

Preface

Inevitably any work of Marxist theory must come into opposition with orthodox economics which rejects its premises and perspectives completely, while apparently dealing with the same issues. I have attempted to reduce these confrontations to a minimum, partly for readers who have not studied the subject, but also because too much attention to economics as it is traditionally defined and taught can only be misleading. Ultimately orthodox economics in all its varieties must be studied as a psycho-pathological symptom, and I have attempted to treat it as nothing more than an accurate theoretical expression of the irrationality of a society whose obscenities it justifies, and then celebrates, as natural and eternal.

The City University, London Geoffrey Kay
June 1978

1 Absolute Poverty

In 1970 the average wage of male workers in Britain was £50 per week, £2,500 per year, which allowed them to enjoy a standard of living their predecessors in the nineteenth century would not have imagined possible. In the same year the average interest rate paid by building societies to investors was just under 7 per cent which was barely sufficient to protect funds from the depredations of inflation. But suppose, for the sake of argument, investors were able to earn 5 per cent in real terms: on this basis it is easy to calculate the minimum capital necessary for a person to earn the equivalent of the average wage without working, was of the order of £50,000. This is only a rough calculation but it tells us something very important about our society, since the distribution of personal wealth is so unequal that only a small percentage of the population has this amount of money. In 1974 the top $3\frac{1}{2}$ per cent of the population owned 87 per cent of the ordinary shares, 94 per cent of other company securities and 96 per cent of all personally owned land. In other words the ownership of *income-yielding assets* is highly concentrated among a very small section of the population, and by this criterion of wealth the vast majority of the population are absolutely poor. They live in *absolute poverty* and are dependent upon work and wages.

Extreme inequality in the ownership of income-yielding wealth is a permanent feature of modern British society. Data from the beginning of this century are not significantly different from more recent figures and there is no evidence to suggest that conditions were significantly different in the nineteenth century. Not that this type of inequality is peculiarly British; with small local variations, it is present throughout the entire capitalist world. Moreover, it is a feature of capitalist society that resists all changes. In the recent past it has survived spectacular economic growth, progressive taxation and many other legislative measures supposed to benefit the poor at the expense of the rich. The reason for this is simple: extreme inequality in the ownership of income-yielding assets is a condition of existence for capitalist society and therefore cannot be changed within its framework. For the existence of wealth in the form of capital – money that yields more money – requires as its counterpart a class of men with no wealth at all, dependent for their livelihood on work and wages. This is the working class.

The absolute poverty of the working class is visibly present in the conditions of work where everything the worker touches belongs to another. The means of production he uses, that is the machines, buildings, materials, etc., all belong to his employer, who also owns the output. The only thing the worker owns is his capacity to work and his economic welfare depends upon his being able to sell this at the best possible price. In the course of this century, particularly during the period of the post-war boom, this price measured in terms of the commodities it can purchase, the real wage, has risen to unprecedented heights, at least in the advanced industrialised countries of the west. As a result of this and the maintenance of full or near full employment backed up by social welfare, the working class has enjoyed greater prosperity and security than at any time in its history. In these circumstances it appears strange to talk of absolute poverty, and the old socialist claim that the working class has nothing to lose but its chains seems an archaic relic of the past when the working class did indeed live in dire poverty. Yet the fact remains that the working class today has no greater economic autonomy than its forbears a hundred years ago.

Consider the situation of a contemporary worker who loses his job. This has happened to several million workers in the industrialised world since the long boom faltered in 1973, not counting the other millions of young people who have never found jobs at all. Many of the workers who have recently suffered unemployment for the first time, earned wages that allowed them to enjoy all the trappings of 'affluence' – decent housing, cars, television, refrigerators and so on. But the loss of the job puts this standard of living immediately in jeopardy, particularly if unemployment lasts for anything more than a few weeks. In the unlikely event of a working class family having a large private income, its initial response to unemployment is to cut back spending on marginal items, and attempt to maintain its style of life intact in the hope that new work will be found shortly. As the period of unemployment lengthens, it begins to eat into savings, but this does not hold out much hope. Working class savings are notoriously low, and often take the form of insurance policies that can only be cashed in at a considerable loss. If the family decides to sell off it consumer durables, apart from reducing its standard of living immediately it will invariably make further losses as second-hand prices are always far below prices for new articles. Moreover, many working class purchases are financed by hire purchase where the interest element makes the actual price higher than the market price, and the family that sells off relatively new items bought in this way often finds that, far from releasing cash, it lands itself in further debt. Working class affluence is entirely dependent upon wages: remove these – i.e. unemployment – and the absolute poverty of its social situation shows through very quickly. In the nineteenth century unemployment meant immediate destitution; the modern worker is clearly much better off than his forbears – for him and his family poverty is a few weeks, maybe even a few months, away.

This picture of modern working class life takes no account of the important innovations made this century in the organisation and provision of social welfare and the development of insurance programmes designed to protect the working class from the depredations of unemployment. According to the official view, the systems of social security that, in one form or another, have been set up in all the advanced industrial countries since the last war, are designed to protect the worker from unemployment and the other economic hazards of modern life, and prevent the absolute poverty of his social situation asserting itself in the way we have just described; and it is true that these systems have alleviated much suffering among the short-term unemployed and those chronically unable to work for one reason or another. But the extent to which they have changed the social relations of capitalist society can be easily exaggerated: already there are definite signs that they cannot cope with large-scale chronic unemployment. It is one thing to manage successfully a social welfare programme when the rate of unemployment runs at about 3 per cent as it did for the thirty years following the Second World War; it is quite different when the rate of unemployment rises and the period out of work goes up from a couple of weeks to several months or even years. Not only does the cost-factor increase, but it does so at the very moment when national economies are under stress and governments are forced to curb public expenditure. The confidence so prevalent in the fifties and sixties, that full employment could be permanently maintained, has waned in the world recession of the seventies, and projections for the rest of the century indicate the possibility of levels of unemployment on the scale of the inter-war period. So far the social security systems have not been faced with problems of this magnitude, but the evidence of the last few years hardly inspires confidence in their ability to manage them. In this light it is hardly an exaggeration to insist that absolute poverty is still a condition of working class life.

Anxiety about the social implications of unemployment payments, openly expressed in conservative circles and tacitly accepted by those further to the left, confirms this perspective. As a result of a combination of circumstances, the level of unemployment and social service benefits rose throughout the fifties and sixties to levels where they allowed a passable standard of living in terms of basic needs. At the same time, a less rapid rise in the wage of low-paid jobs, together with anomalies in the taxation system, cut into the premium on work. In extreme cases it actually pays a worker to become unemployed rather than to take a job; in many cases it makes working barely worthwhile. Take the example of a worker who can earn £60 per week, which, after deductions, gives him a take-home pay of £50. If he can get £40 a week in unemployment and social security benefits, the net reward for working is only £10, which is hardly an inducement to do a dull and monotonous job. Given the decline of the puritan ethic which valued work for its own sake, it is hardly surprising that the call to widen the differential between unemployment pay and low wages has grown in urgency and stridency. For the fact is that whatever the ideological terms in which this call is made, it reflects a fundamental condition of capitalist society – that work is imposed upon the working-class as a necessity. The universal application of the principles of social welfare, so that any member of the community has the right to benefits sufficient to maintain an average standard of living, would rapidly undermine capitalism by immediately alleviating absolute poverty and relieving the working class of its dependence upon wage-labour. There is no doubt that the guardians of the modern state are fully aware of this, even if their perceptions are hidden behind cant about incentives and mealy-mouthed appeals to social responsibility.

If we put aside the moralism that invariably surrounds this issue we find another case in favour of the necessity of work. Its starting point is that work is essential in any form of society, since things cannot be consumed which have not been previously produced. The necessity to work, this argument continues, is therefore a natural or material condition of social life which the relations of capitalist production – absolute poverty and the dependence of the working class on wage-labour – do not create but merely translate into a social form. Like many false arguments, this one is compelling because it rests upon a half or distorted truth. Instead of work we should say that social life is dependent upon the expenditure of *productive labour*, meaning in this context that labour which produces items that are useful and necessary to maintain the standard of life. Clearly that section of the community which does not work at all but lives off unearned income, does not perform productive labour in this or any other sense, but there are also many people who do work but who do not labour productively. In feudal society, to take a case where prejudice does not obscure the issue as it

Absolute Poverty

does with our own, the activities of retainers illustrates the distinction clearly. Part of the functions of this group was to control the serfs and make certain that they delivered part of their product each year to their vassal as dues. No doubt they worked hard at what was a thankless task but the fact of the matter is that however hard they worked their efforts were unproductive in the sense that they made no contribution whatsoever to producing items of consumption that satisfied needs. What they did was to ensure that production took place in a feudal framework. The real producers of wealth were serfs who paid tribute to their vassals. Clearly this was a necessary function for feudalism, but one that cannot be judged necessary on natural or material grounds.

Although not so clearly defined, the feudal retainer has many counterparts in capitalist society. Many workers do jobs that make no direct contribution to material production, such as bank-workers, accountants, civil servants and the like, although their efforts are indispensable to capitalism. There are other workers who do labour productively, but who would do so differently if they were not subjected to the dictates of capitalism: for example, workers who duplicate each others' efforts because of competition; the attempt to differentiate identical products by styling and packaging; or the building of accelerated obsolescence into products to maintain market turnover. The question of who is and who is not productive is a highly charged issue, but it is sufficient for our purpose merely to establish that such a distinction exists. The point we need to make is that the vast development of technology during the period of industrial capitalism, that began around the beginning of the last century, has increased productivity faster than social needs have been allowed to grow, and reduced productive labour accordingly. The pace of innovation has, if anything, speeded up this century, and the introduction of micro-electronics promises an even sharper fall in the amount of productive labour that will be necessary by the end of the century.

Increased productivity can be used to improve living standards, as in part it has. It can also be used to reduce working time, and this too has happened. But if the increases in productivity already achieved, let alone those in the pipeline, were used exclusively for these ends, the social fabric of capitalism would be rapidly torn apart, since the rise in living standards would sharply reduce the necessity to work. The point is this: the social relations of capitalist production which compel the working class into wage-labour have never been materially determined in the way the argument we have summarised claims. What we can say is that in the nineteenth century, when social productivity was much lower than it is today, and most work was in consequence productive labour in the sense we have defined it here, the social relations of production that compelled the working class into wage-labour were powerfully reinforced by material scarcity. But this is no longer true, at least not to the same extent. The revolution in productivity has torn the social relations of production away from their material moorings, so that the need for the vast majority of the population to spend by far the greater part of their waking life at work merely to earn enough to be able to live, no longer reflects the material conditions and possibilities of production.

To return to the early factory system of the nineteenth century as a point of comparison; then the absolute poverty of the newly formed working class was immediately reproduced in the level of its wages and its standard of living. Today, absolute poverty remains, but wages and living standards are so much higher. What does this tell us? That the process that has produced this vast material wealth has simultaneously reproduced absolute poverty; that it has produced this wealth only on condition of absolute poverty. From the outset it is necessary for us to understand this double nature of capitalist production that, as it produces massive wealth on the one side, it must reproduce scarcity and absolute poverty for the mass of the people on the other. As the world capitalist economy once again slides into a traditional crisis, not because too little has been produced to satisfy human needs, but because too much production has threatened the basis of scarcity, this contradiction between wealth and poverty asserts itself in typical forms. Once again a society based upon the necessity of wage-labour can no longer offer work, particularly to the new recruits to its labour-force. The measures that governments throughout the western world are adopting to cope with this particular problem reveal the senselessness of the situation with stark clarity – a proliferation of meaningless activities under the rubric of work experience, the creation of unnecessary problems and the attempt at necessarily ineffectual solutions. Like the astronomers of old who believed the earth was the centre of the universe and were forced to create ever more elaborate cosmographies to accommodate data to the opposite theory, the political managers of contemporary capitalist society, and the economists and social scientists who support them with 'expert' advice, find it increasingly difficult to reconcile the dogma that capitalism is a rational system for the conduct of human affairs with what is going on around them.

2 The Elements of Economic Theory

In this chapter we assemble the elements of economic theory and examine material production and basic reproduction, money, commodities and value.

1. MATERIAL PRODUCTION AND BASIC REPRODUCTION

Material production consists of the actions men take upon nature in their efforts to humanise it; to turn natural objects of little or no use in their raw state into forms where they can satisfy human needs. Hollowing out a tree to make a canoe is a primitive example; using tin, rubber, iron, coal and so on to make a car is more complex; but the principle is the same in both cases. Both the canoe and the car are *products* – natural objects modified by *labour* (i.e. purposive human activity) to satisfy some need. A definition of production in these terms as a human process where men confront nature with their labour is the only rational basis from which economic theory can begin, but in capitalist society whose organisation, forms, practices and ends are irrational, even this basic definition is swept to one side.

The grounds of this irrationality, in practice and in theory, are the *instruments of production* that men place between themselves and the natural objects of their labour; simple implements, tools and machines ranging from the primitive axehead to the most advanced computerised system. Throughout recorded history, at least, the producers who shape final products have always made use of instruments of one sort or another and production has never been a simple labour process. But instruments of production are themselves products – natural objects modified by labour – and the only rational way to understand their contribution to production is to treat them as such. The process of production is then defined as a *complex labour process*, which requires not only the *living labour* of the final or direct producers, but also the labour spent previously making instruments, variously called *dead, past* or *dated labour*. But, however complex it becomes with the growth in the ratio of dead to living labour, production remains a labour process where the ultimate agents are nature and men. Orthodox economics that reproduces in theory the irrationalities of capitalist production, in practice rejects this position and defines instruments as a separate and independent factor of production called 'capital' – a third party that is the equivalent of the other two. All its errors and mystifications originate in this nonsense which is a faithful reflection of a society pathologically incapable of distinguishing human beings from natural materials and inanimate objects.

The conditions that induce this illusion of a third factor of production are fully developed in capitalist society.

(i) The instruments of production characteristically assume the form of machinery whose operations are independent of the strength of the living worker and his skill. With a tool the living producer is still the active agent since it is his skill and energy which determines the pace and quality of production; but with machines developed in capitalist society the situation is reversed, and it is the instrument that determines the process of production.

(ii) The labour that uses machines is seldom, if ever, the labour that makes them; nor are the two groups of producers necessarily known to each other as they work not only in different places but at different times. Within the confines of a factory the instruments of production have the same objective existence as the living workers, and empirical evidence confirms their autonomy of labour. But this is an indictment of empiricism that takes appearances at face value, rather than proof that machines are equivalent to labour.

(iii) The producers do not own the instruments of production which have social as well as technical autonomy from labour. Moreover, the impression of their independence of labour, and productive equivalence to it, is reinforced by a system of payment which makes profits look like the reward for the contribution made to production by 'capital' and wages the reward for the parallel contribution of labour.

But none of these conditions, taken singly or together, alters in the slightest way the fundamental nature of production as a complex labour process. What they show, particularly the third condition, is the extent to which capitalism perverts production and stands it on its head, and it is on these grounds that we criticise it, and not just the theories that accept it, as an irrational form of society.

We must be absolutely clear that the definition of production as a

The Elements of Economic Theory

complex labour process does not require measuring the amount of labour a product requires on the one side, nor does it imply that the prices of products are proportionate to this amount on the other. It is easy to demonstrate the practical impossibility of the former: one would have to discover not only how much living labour was required but how much dead labour as well, and since instruments of production are produced with the use of instruments of production, this endeavour would soon disappear on a trail that leads into the mists of prehistory. As regards the latter, there is no evidence to suggests that prices are proportionate to labour. But in neither case is the definition of production as a complex labour process challenged in the slightest degree. The remaining criticism open to the economists is self-destructive: the starting point of economics, they claim, is relative prices, and since the definition of production as a complex labour process cannot, on its own admission, make a direct contribution to this, another operationally more useful definition is required. But as any other definition is irrational, this line of reasoning only proves that relative prices cannot be the starting point of economic theory, or that if they are made so the theory must be as irrational as the society it purports to analyse.

Before moving on we must note that calling the instruments of production 'capital' is hardly less misleading than defining them as an independent factor of production. Since men have made use of instruments from the earliest times, this piece of nomenclature immediately defines all history as capitalist history: feudalism is conceived as underdeveloped capitalism and communism is inconceivable being seen either as an updated or inefficient version of capitalism, depending upon the prejudices of the individual. History is reduced to the single dimension of technical change and is nothing more than the history of objects. We must reject this and all other forms of vulgar materialism.

In so far as the immediate result of the process of production, the product, satisfies a human need, it is a means of consumption. Thus consumption is the end of production; but in its turn consumption is just as necessary to production. Nothing can be consumed that is not previously produced; but equally production cannot occur without prior consumption. The appropriate technique for analysing the chain of events that links production and consumption as mutual subjects and predicates, is the circuit: $P-C-P-C\ldots$, where P represents production and C consumption. But consumption here is not total but *necessary consumption*, the consumption necessary to maintain the prevailing level of production. This consumption has two components:

the *personal consumption* of the living producers, in capitalist society the working class; and the depreciation of the instruments of production. This is called *productive consumption* since it refers to consumption that takes place within the process of production. The circuit that contains production and necessary consumption is called the *circuit of basic reproduction* since it describes the activities necessary to maintain a society at any given level of development. The chain of events this circuit embraces must be present in every society, though its form of organisation varies as well as the way it is linked together. In capitalist society the link is organised through money to which we turn in the next section.

First we must note that in every society known to the historian production has regularly exceeded necessary consumption by an amount that is known as *surplus production* or simply *surplus*. In capitalist society surplus production is larger and more systematic than any other, yet the idea is completely absent from orthodox economics, and this is significant lacuna. If we apply the category of necessary consumption to capitalist society, we would include the wages of productive labour and the depreciation of equipment and materials, but exclude profit for the simple reason that profits, and the class which they support, are not technically necessary for production. This is hardly a palatable position for economists who treat the capitalist world as though it were the best of all possible worlds and the capitalist class as a heroic entity morally entitled to everything it gets. Thus national income accounts not only exclude profits from the netting factor (i.e. necessary consumption) but to be strictly fair and impartial they exclude wages as well, and treat both categories as though they were part of the surplus. Mystification assumes new dimensions of confusion when it is expressed in neatly printed pages of 'objective' statistics.

These introductory notes, it must be stressed, are of a very general nature and tell us nothing directly about the nature of capitalist society and how it works, and should be treated only as broad guidelines to the theory that follows.

2. MONEY

The most striking feature of capitalist society is the universality of money. All products (whether they are intended for personal or productive consumption) are exchanged directly for money, or indirectly through taxes and insurance contributions. Natural objects, especially land, which are freely available to society and have no cost of production, can

The Elements of Economic Theory

also command a price; and even human attributes, most notably the capacity to work, are bought and sold for money. It is this universal exchangeability of money, a condition created by capitalist society, that lies at the root of the illusion that all things human and non-human are equivalents, for the fact is that in capitalist society money makes everything the equivalent of everything else. Where a product is traded in this way it is called a *commodity*. The commodity is the simple cell of capitalist society but this fact is veiled by the golden mists of money. A few remarks are therefore necessary about the nature of money.

Money is difficult to analyse not because it is strange and esoteric, but because it is commonplace and familiar. Common sense alone seems to be all that is required, but it is inadequate and misleading. All that it can validly tell us is that we are dealing with a most paradoxical phenomenon; one which is of little or no use in itself but is everywhere desired and accepted as the stuff of wealth. If we search the annals of monetary history, we would not find a fully developed monetary system in which a generally useful item has served as money. The materials most commonly used for this purpose have been precious stones, silver and, above all, gold, and none is particularly important as a means of production or as an item of personal consumption. On the other hand, their physical properties make them suitable as a medium of exchange: they are durable, easily divided into small amounts, or aggregated into large quantities, and convenient in so far as their scarcity makes them valuable and a small quantity in terms of weight can represent a large consignment of commodities. But as items of direct use in either production or consumption they have little significance. This is readily understandable: money, as such, never enters into consumption, but merely passes from hand to hand, so that if a generally useful item were used as money a conflict would arise between this use and the other purposes which it could serve. We can find no solution to the paradox of money by examining its material form, since it only restates the problem of an item of little use emerging as the acknowledged representative of wealth. In modern society, where money is represented by paper, the paradox is fully developed, and the illusion once popular in the nineteenth century, that the nature of gold made money, is now without any substantial basis. Thus to begin the analysis of money with its material substance is to put the cart before the horse: only when we have understood the nature of money as such can we grasp its paradox and see why its material substance has only marginal use or no use at all.

Economists believe they have a plausible solution to this paradox. Money, they argue, is a convention developed to overcome the inconvenience of direct barter, where an individual has to find a customer who not only wants the commodity he is selling, but who, in turn, wishes to sell the commodity he wants to buy. The introduction of money eases the situation considerably since it allows a sale to be made to one person and a purchase to be made from another, without all the rigamarole of direct trading. What is necessary is the general acceptability of the item that acts as money. This developed slowly so that the early forms of money were commodities highly prized in themselves. But as the experience of monetary circulation develops, the merely convenient nature of money asserts itself until it becomes possible to supercede what is called commodity-money altogether, and replace it with *fiat* money – 'worthless' pieces of paper – which does the job equally well. As one economist admits, this is a stylized bit of history, but one that appears to account for the nature of money as we know it today. The core of this argument is that money is nothing more than a convention designed to facilitate exchange, with no intrinsic importance of its own. It is prized only because it gives access to things of real worth, but to do this it need not be useful itself. The paradox is resolved, and in a very comforting fashion. For, according to this account of things, money is simply a rational device that allows men to get on with the real business of life, the production and distribution of real wealth to satisfy needs, in an efficient fashion. Disproving this view is no simple task: first, because it appears to account for the facts of everyday experience; second, it reinforces the common belief that whatever might be wrong with the world, it is organised on a fundamentally rational basis; and third, because the alternative explanation is one of the most complex pieces of economic theory ever developed. But if money is simply the convenience that the economists tell us, we have to face a paradox no less daunting than the original one: why, we can legitimately ask, has this convenience proved itself so inconvenient by precipitating so many major crises in recent economic history?

The question we have to answer is a fundamental one, and, for this reason, deceptively simple – what is money? The temptation is to follow the line of the economists and attempt to deduce the nature of money from its function as the medium of exchange – i.e. money is what money does. But this stands things on their heads, for we can never understand the nature of anything simply by looking at its functions. For example, the function of a ladder is to allow us to climb up a wall, but armed with this information we know surprisingly little about what a ladder is. If, on the other hand, we defined a ladder as two parallel rods joined by a number of slats strong enough to take a person's weight, we would know what a

The Elements of Economic Theory

ladder is and have sufficient information to deduce its functions. The function of a thing follows from its nature, and although common sense suggests the opposite, and this is usually sufficient for dealing with the practicalities of everyday life, science must reproduce the correct sequence of events and begin with the nature of phenomena. This does not mean that the functions should be ignored since they offer vital clues and prevent enquiries spinning off into an vacuum. Thus in asking the question, 'what is the nature of money?', we will bear in mind that one of its main functions is the mediation of exchange.

When a commodity is bought and sold, the money received or spent upon it represents its *price*. This proposition, which we will see is more complex than it first appears, suggests a line of analysis which we must eschew. That is to say, it suggests that we should straight away look into the factors which determine the price, (i.e. the *magnitude* of price), of an individual commodity; but for reasons that will become clear later and cannot be anticipated here, it would be quite wrong to move in that direction. Let us take the second, though less obvious approach and consider the total of aggregated prices; in other words, the total amount of money circulating in a society for a given period, say a year. If we take out all possible causes of double-counting, for example where commodities are bought and sold twice, total prices must in some sense (which we have yet to discover) be equal to the total volume of commodities produced and traded. The reason for this equality is obvious enough: the buying and selling of commodities changes their ownership but does not add to their volume in any way. Exchange transactions merely move round the mass of commodities that production has brought into existence so that these transactions added up on the one side must equal the mass of commodities on the other. What is less obvious is the nature of this equality and whether it can properly be called an equality at all.

Consider a balance sheet on which these transactions are recorded. On the left-hand side is a list of all the commodities sold – the cloth, the corn, the cars, the refrigerators and so on, listed individually; on the right-hand side, the price at which each one is bought and sold. This list would be unmanageably long but this is the least of the problems. If we group individual commodities and then consolidate them to two, all the fundamental difficulties of the analysis of exchange and money still remain. The following schema represents just such a simplification:

Commodities	*Prices*
10 tons of iron	£2,000
1,000 yards of cloth	£1,000

The problems it presents are perfectly obvious: we can calculate the total of prices on the right-hand side easily enough – i.e. £3,000; but how do we add the left-hand side together? And if we could find some unit in which to express the iron and the cloth to get a total, in what sense, if any, could we say that this total is equal to £3,000?

Stripped down to these elementary dimensions, it appears that all we have here is a simple puzzle and the fact that no solution is ready at hand makes it appear, moreover, a trivial one. But as we have just seen, the scale on which we express the problem is irrelevant since it exists wherever there is more than one commodity. But more importantly, there has to be a sense in which the total on the left side equals that on the right, even though we do not know how to total the left; and even if we did it would be in different units to those on the right. Equality of some sort exists because these prices have exchanged these commodities. It is given by the very nature of exchange – every child knows that 5 pennies *equal*, say, 10 sweets.

When two or more things are equal to each other this means either they are identical to each other in every respect, or that they possess some factor in common in equal amounts. Where the equation takes the form 10 tons of iron + 1,000 yards of cloth = £3,000, equality must be of the second sort because the elements of the equation are obviously not identical. More generally, whenever we bring two phenomena of different types together into a quantitative relationship to obtain a result such as adding together iron and cloth to get a total, we must again presuppose some common quality, though this time it need not be present in equal amounts. The problem of exchange as we have posed it here thus resolves itself into two questions: first, what is it that iron and cloth (and by implication every other commodity) have in common? and, second, what is it that commodities have in common with money?

The first of these questions is relatively simple and we already have the answer. Suppose the 10 tons of iron and the 1,000 yards of cloth represent the annual output of society: the end result of the process of material production. It has been achieved by men using various instruments of production on materials we assume are found freely in nature. During the course of the year a definite number of man hours are expended by living labour and a quantity of instruments are used up which require another definite amount of man hours of labour to replace. The labour currently spent by living workers is qualitatively no different from that spent earlier by other workers who make instruments of production, so that the two types can be added together, and when this is done we are close to getting the total we want. If we add together the

The Elements of Economic Theory   15

living plus the dead labour required to produce the iron to that required for the cloth, we have it: it is the sum of four elements all designated in the same units, man hours or labour time – two lots of dead labour plus two of living.

Two objections can be made to the basis of this calculation which we must mention though neither carries any weight. The first is the practical impossibility, already conceded, of measuring the amount of labour that goes into a commodity, so that this calculation is impossible in practice. But a phenomenon does not cease to exist in definite amounts and have definite quantitative effects which can be perceived and calibrated simply because of the difficulties of direct measurement. In fact, if we take a commodity it is impossible to tell by direct examination whether it contains any labour at all, let alone how much. If we stripped a car down to its components or unravelled a scarf we would not find an atom of labour, yet this does not stop us from knowing that they are both the products of labour. The second objection is that different commodities are produced by different kinds of labour, and that the four blocs of labour we have added together here are really four different types of labour – one labour that weaves cloth; a second that makes looms; a third that smelts iron and a fourth that makes smelters: and for this reason they cannot be added together any more than the original commodities. But we also know that labour can be switched from one activity to the next: in the case of unskilled labour very quickly, and in the case of skilled labour after a period of retraining. In what the economists call the long-run, one type of labour can be turned into any other; so that any one particular type of labour is in one sense only a temporary form of labour-in-general or *abstract labour* – a phenomenon we will examine more closely later. All we need to remark here is that there are no conceptual obstacles to treating different commodities such as iron and cloth as embodiments of definite amounts of labour and then adding them together to get a total for the left-hand column.

Suppose this total comes to 5,000 hours of labour; the proportions in which it is distributed between the iron and the cloth are absolutely irrelevant to our second question; what is it that commodities have in common with money? What is it that 5,000 hours of labour have in common with £3,000? We have now reduced our equation down to this form: 5,000 hours of labour = £3,000. Expressed this way the question is impossible to answer for the formula applied above, that non-identical phenomena that are in some respect equal must share a common property and possess it in the same amounts, does not apply. Certainly it does not apply when we are dealing with inconvertible paper money (i.e.

not convertible into a commodity such as gold) for it is stretching the analysis beyond credulity to claim that banknotes are a product of labour and that it takes the same amount of time to print £3,000 as it does to smelt 10 tons of iron and weave 1,000 yards of cloth. All the same, labour must be the basis of this equality, because every individual commodity is equal to money and the only thing commodities have in common among themselves is labour.

The difficulty we are facing becomes less intractable once we understand that it applies with particular force only when we are dealing with fully developed inconvertable paper money. Let us move one step backwards in the development of money, both historically and logically, to a situation where the material substance of money was a commodity like any other – gold. Gold, of course, is a natural phenomenon but its discovery, processing and transportation make it a product like any other, while its exchangeability makes it a commodity. This step does not take us very far back into history for in the last century gold coins were in general circulation and it is only since 1971, when the official gold-dollar parity was abandoned, that all the world currencies did not ultimately find their basis in gold through their exchangeability with the dollar. By this time, however, the connection between money and gold had become tenuous; nevertheless it is an important reminder that completely inconvertible paper money is only a very recent development and one whose extremely short history is not characterised by a high degree of stability.

Where the circulating medium consists exclusively of gold or paper convertible into gold, at least a part of the problem posed by the equation is solved, in as much as money is a commodity it can be brought into relation with other commodities as the product of labour. But this still leaves the problem of quantity unresolved since it is unlikely that a gold coin ever exchanged for a commodity that took the same labour time to produce as the coin itself. However before we turn to this aspect of the question we have some extremely complex problems to handle and need an analogy to help us on our way.

Suppose I wish to weigh a loaf of bread using a pair of old-fashioned scales: I put the loaf on one side and pieces of iron on the other until the two sides are in balance, at which point the balancing of the scales tells me that the bread and the iron possess something in common, weight, and this in equal amounts. What is the relationship between the bread and iron when they are on the scales? Although I could alternate their position and use the bread to weigh iron, when they are on the scales in the conventional way they play distinct roles: the bread relates its weight to the iron and the iron expresses the weight of the bread. If someone were to ask me what the weight of the bread was, I would tell him 'these pieces of iron'; and if he asked me to give him the weight of the bread I would pass him the iron. Of course the iron pieces are not really the weight of the bread – this is a physical property of the bread and inseparable from it. They are the equivalent of the weight of the bread, what is called the *equivalent form* of the weight. In other words, the weight of the bread has found a second form in which to exist outside the bread and independently of it, and this new form is as significant as the original one.

When a commodity is 'weighed' against money – an event analogous to the weighing of an item like bread – the money represents the labour in the commodity just as the iron represents the weight of the bread; and it becomes the form of existence of that labour in the same way as the iron becomes the form of existence of the bread. *Money is the equivalent form of labour as it is embodied in commodities.* But the matter we put aside a moment ago, that iron only expresses the weight of the bread because it contains weight like the bread and, moreover, is the same weight, must now be recognised since it appears to invalidate this approach and to take us back to square one. For surely the logic of this analogy is that money can only act as the equivalent form of the labour embodied in a commodity if it also is a commodity that embodies labour and, moreover, the same amount of labour. The fact that this is not so is what creates the problem of money in the first place. But our position is not as bad as it seems.

It is true that in a primitive economy, where exchange occurs only occasionally and money is not thoroughly established as a medium of exchange, anyone selling a commodity will only accept in return another containing the same amount of labour. The uncertainty attached to money in this situation obliges him to treat it as a final payment for his commodity and he must be prepared to hold it indefinitely as though it were a permanent form of wealth. But in capitalist society, where money is firmly established as the medium of exchange, the situation is different. In some circumstances, even here, money acts as a means of final payment and is acceptable only in a substantive form that embodies labour time, but generally speaking, this is not the case. As the medium of exchange it is in constant circulation, changing hands all the time, so that for any one individual it is never more than a temporary form of wealth. The more complete the development of money as the medium of exchange, and the more it becomes only a temporary form of holding wealth, the more the material substance of money diminishes in importance. As a medium of exchange it matters less to an individual whether what he receives as money contains the same labour as the commodity he sells, than that it should represent this labour and demonstrate this to be the case by allowing him to buy a roughly equivalent commodity from a third party. In these circumstances, the material substance of money is increasingly determined by the convenience of exchange, until it becomes only a symbolic representation.

Consider the development of coins. Prior to their general use, the appropriate physical amount of the money-commodity had to be present in every transaction which, in effect, meant weighing out gold-dust, silver or whatever – a practice that was not only inconvenient, but prone to all kinds of fraud and cheating. Coinage overcomes this by officially designating weight, and the first coins must have contained the amount of specie imprinted on them. But this parity is intrinsically unstable and has built into it a tendency for coins to depreciate below their face value. The wear and tear of circulation alone tends to reduce the weight of coins below their official weight: but more important is the power of the issuing body to clip and debase the coinage to a point where the parity becomes merely nominal, and the replacement of coins by paper a short logical step. In other words, we can see in the development of coinage the decisive rupture between the nominal and the real value of money of which today's paper money is the logical outcome. But this development, it must be stressed, does not change the fundamental nature of money at all: it merely changes its material form in a way that makes it more suitable as a medium of exchange. There is a further development in progress at the moment as paper money itself is increasingly substituted by credit cards. Were it to disappear altogether in favour of plastic cards and records stored in some central computer, nothing fundamental would be changed and money would remain what it always has been – the equivalent form of the labour time embodied in commodities.

We have now reached our conclusion and for all practical purposes the problem is solved. The greatest difficulty in understanding what money is arises from the development of the material form that is most suitable for its function as the medium of exchange. This is not the only function of money but it is the one that has shaped its physical development. As the medium of exchange money is in constant circulation, and because individuals never hold it for very long it can be symbolically represented by pieces of otherwise worthless paper. Those economists who take this function as their starting point conclude that money by its very nature is nothing but a convenience and a symbol, and although this approach appears to account for most of the facts, it has actually stood things on their head. The correct sequence of events is this: (1) the nature of money is that it is the equivalent form of the labour-time embodied in commodities just as pieces of iron can become the equivalent form of the weight of objects; (2) because it is the equivalent form of the labour-time embodied in commodities and all commodities possess labour-time as a common factor, money becomes the common factor of commodities and can therefore function as a medium of circulating them; (3) as such, money serves as a convenience giving rise to the illusion that it is nothing more than a symbolic convention.

Nobody would claim that we could understand the nature of time by examining clocks, or that it had changed as digital watches have superceded sun-dials. In the same way, it is absurd to attempt an explanation of the nature of money through changes in its material form from lumps of gold in one period to electronic impulses in the memory banks of a computer in another. In fact, the contrary is the case: the material forms that money assumes cloud its nature in a mist that gets denser with each development of these forms until it becomes as opaque as it is today. Thus, returning to our example, to claim that 10 tons of iron and 1,000 yards of cloth equal £3,000 and therefore share some common property with it, appears nonsense if we think of this £3,000 as so many pieces of paper: but it becomes perfectly comprehensible once we understand that paper is only the material form of money which is the equivalent form of existence of the labour-time embodied in commodities.

Aside from purely theoretical interest, the demystification of money and its resolution into the equivalent form of the labour-time embodied in commodities has the most practical implications for our study. In the first place it shows that human activity, i.e. labour, is still the real basis of economic life even in a world bound in a web of money. It is all too easy to take capitalist society at face value and get so lost in its monetary miasma that the indisputable statement that it rests upon the activity of men reproducing the conditions of life seems at worst false and at best abstract and irrelevant. At the same time, the universality of money makes its comprehension vital if we are to understand anything of the nature of capitalist society. It might seem in blatant contradiction to what we have just said to insist that it is indeed money and its own peculiar logic that forms the basis of capitalism, but this is a contradiction of capitalism itself which our theory only expresses. To say that money is the basis of capitalist society and labour merely one of its features, is not an inverted consciousness of the world as it is now, but a true consciousness of a world that is itself inverted. We live in a world where obvious truths appear fantastic precisely because they are fantastic; where the need for men to develop themselves into full human beings appears a secondary consideration to the calculus of money, because it is a secondary consideration. In other words, we live in a world ruled not by labour and the needs it generates, but by its abstract, surrogate and equivalent form of being; by money; not by simple money, however, but money evolved into a monstrous caricature of itself – capital.

3. VALUE AND LABOUR

Before we start the analysis of capital, we must extend our vocabulary to include the concept of value which has been implicit in all we have said so far without being mentioned explicitly.

We have seen that a commodity is, in the first place, a product shaped by labour to satisfy some human need: in this respect it is a *use-value*. There is little we need to say here beyond noting that it is the nature of a commodity as a thing – as a blanket, a car, a computer or whatever – that makes it a use-value, and that as use-values, therefore, commodities necessarily differ from each other. It is from these differences that the reason for exchange arises – one particular type of use-value, say a coat, for another which is different, say 10 yards of linen. In addition to having value-in-use, commodities also have value-in-exchange, or *exchange-value*. What distinguishes a commodity from a simple product is that commodities are always exchanged and never consumed directly by those who produce them: they never find their way from producer to consumer directly – by tribute, immediate appropriation or some form of collectivist distribution. This exchange can take the form of simple barter where commodities are exchanged directly, but in capitalist society it invariably involves an exchange against money. Thus all commodities, no matter how different they are as use-values, become the same as exchange-values: when they are expressed for money, the qualitative differences among them disappear in favour of differences of a purely quantitative nature. Thus blankets, cars, computers, etc. are all qualitatively different as use-values but when they are exchanged and become exchange-values, these differences disappear and are replaced by differences in quantity. That is to say, as exchange values they are all the same, all money, but different sums of money – so much money for the blanket, a different amount for the car, yet another amount for the computer and so on. Thus the transformation of commodities into exchange-values stamps them with a common character which then becomes the basis of exchange. The substance of this common character cannot be found in their use-value, in their physical or *natural forms*, for in this respect they differ from each other; it is to be discovered in their social form, in the fact that they are all the products of social labour. Under this guise they are all made of the same stuff and share the common property of being *value*.

We must be absolutely clear from the start that value is not the same as what is commonly called price. When we say a commodity has value we mean two things: first, that it has been produced by labour, and second, it has been produced by a definite amount of labour. In the first respect commodities are all the same; in the second they differ from each other quantitatively. There is a strong temptation to take this quantitative variation as the basis of prices and argue that the rate at which commodities actually exchange for each other, relative prices, is proportionate to their values, to the amount of labour they embody. But such a conclusion would be premature and, as it turns out, incorrect. Later we shall see why this is the case: for the present we will concentrate on value as such.

It is true, as we have already mentioned, that the amount of labour embodied in a commodity cannot be measured in practice and to this extent we cannot measure the value of individual commodities. On the other hand, it would be absurd to conclude from this that commodities do not embody definite amounts of labour and have definite values, and that these magnitudes, although impossible to state precisely, do not play a vital part in determining the structure and development of the capitalist economy. Although we cannot measure the value of a commodity, we can nonetheless state that it is equal to the total labour necessary to produce it, which is the sum of the living labour engaged in its production and the dead labour that made the means of production consumed in its manufacture. The qualification we have slipped in here, that the value of a commodity is determined by the amount of labour necessary for its production, or to be more accurate we should say *socially necessary*, is important for three reasons. First, it allows us to distinguish between the amount of labour that a particular individual or firm may expend in producing a given commodity from the average (or social) amount expended by a group of individuals or firms, and therefore it frees us from the anomaly that inefficiently produced commodities have greater value than those produced more efficiently simply because they take longer to make. The value of a commodity is determined by the amount of labour that is on average necessary for its production. Second, this average can itself vary with the development of technology, so that whenever the amount of labour required on average to produce a commodity falls the value of that commodity falls. Third, the use of the qualification *social* indicates that the value of a commodity is determined not only by the average level of productivity in the industry that produces it, but also by conditions in other branches of the economy. Thus, for example, improved efficiency in the steel industry which reduces the amount of labour needed to make a ton of steel has general repercussions and reduces the value of all commodities that use steel. To sum up: commodities have value because they are produced by labour; and the magnitude of their value is determined by the amount of labour socially necessary for their production.

So much is relatively straightforward but a substantial difficulty is lurking in the wings. When we say all commodities are the same in so far as they are the products of labour, we are tacitly claiming, or so it appears, that labour is all the same. But a cursory glance at the productive process tells us that many different types of labour are involved, not only skilled and unskilled, but many different varieties of each. What is potentially even more damaging to this notion is that the variations in labour correspond closely to variations in use-value – i.e. one type of labour, weaving, produces linen and another altogether different type, tailoring, produces coats. We have already argued that use-value cannot be the basis of exchange since this basis comprises the common factor of commodities, and use-value varies from one commodity to the next. But surely, the critic may retort, labour must be disqualified as the common factor of commodities and the substance of value on exactly the same grounds, since although all commodities are the products of labour, they are the products of different kinds of labour. You can, if you wish, the critic may say, proceed on the assumption that labour is the substance of value and see where this takes you, but you cannot claim that labour is actually the substance of value because all commodities are produced by different types of labour. The resolution of this issue is crucial, since the nature of value and therefore the whole of economic theory pivots upon it.

We have already given a partial answer to this line of criticism in pointing out the possibility of labour switching from one activity to another. At any given moment labour is distributed among the various branches of the economy, engaging in particular activities and turning out a given pattern of use-values. This distribution is not permanently fixed, since workers can be moved from one area to the next, how quickly and efficiently depending upon the degree of skill and the training required. This suggests that all the different types of what we must call *concrete labour*, specific labour performing varied tasks – tailoring here, weaving there – is nevertheless a part of social labour. In other words, although each type of labour is specific, it is nevertheless part of the general labour of society, and in this sense, and this sense only, different types of labour are the same, and are what is called *abstract labour*. But in a society whose products take the form of commodities, all concrete labour would still be abstract labour, i.e. particular parts of social labour, even if there was no movement of producers from one activity to another.

Consider the situation where there are only two commodities, coats and linen. Each is made by a particular type of concrete labour, tailoring in the case of coats, weaving in the case of linen. In trade, coats exchange for linen directly, or indirectly through money; either way does not matter here. What does this exchange mean? A tailor makes a coat and then exchanges it for a definite amount of linen, say 10 yards – the exact amount is immaterial here as we are not concerned with the rules that govern the ratio of exchange. In other words, the tailor has, by expending a particular type of concrete labour, acquired a product, linen, made by another and quite different of type of concrete labour. The sequence of events is this:

tailoring —— 1 coat —— 10 yards of linen —— weaving

giving us a chain which has tailoring at one end and weaving at the other. Just as the coat becomes the equivalent of 10 yards of linen in exchange, so the concrete labour that makes the coat, the labour of the tailor, becomes equivalent to that which makes the linen, the labour of the weaver. Where all products are bought and sold as commodities it is possible for a tailor to acquire the product of any and every type of labour by making and selling coats, just as much as if he produced all these commodities himself. One type of concrete labour is the equivalent of every other type of concrete labour because it is the means of acquiring the product of every other type of concrete labour – but clearly this is only possible because of the system of exchange itself.

The main obstacle to understanding here lies in the terms 'concrete' and 'abstract'; these are rarely used in this way, but usually carry the connotation of real and unreal. The use of term 'concrete' to describe particular types of labour may seem curious, but presents no serious difficulty. It is 'abstract' labour and its relation to concrete labour that really creates the difficulty. The most obvious interpretation is that abstract labour is the essence of concrete labour, the expenditure of muscle, nerves and energy, of which all concrete labour consists. But in this sense abstract labour is unreal, being nothing more than a mental category in the way that mammal is a mental category in relation to cats and dogs – nobody has ever seen or touched a mammal as such! We can get round the difficulty by using the terms 'individual' and 'social' in which the same perspectives can be expressed in more readily understandable ways.

Instead of concrete let us talk of individual labour, and use social in place of abstract labour.

Social labour relates to an aspect of reality which can be readily identified: it is the whole labour force of a society seen as a collective and interdependent force, as a team. Individual labour is performed by the separate individuals who make up this team; but even if we imagine an extreme situation where every individual works alone, producing his own particular brand of commodity and never coming into contact with anybody else while at work, there is nonetheless a sense in which he is part of the collective labour force. This arises first of all from the division of labour and the conditions of material production. Take the tailor again. He works alone in his own shop making coats; but he can only do this if some other individual has woven the wool whose work, in turn, is dependent upon someone else having washed and spun the wool, and so on back to the farmer who tended and reared the sheep. In other words, the tailor is part of a productive team despite the fact he works alone, as do all the other members of the team who never meet each other directly to talk about and plan their work. But the coat is in a very real sense the product of their combined labours, and while everyone is labouring alone at his own individual (concrete) labour, at the same time he is part of the collective labour force performing social (abstract) labour. But how do the individual members of this team who never meet at work forge themselves into a collective unit; how do they relate to each other? Unconsciously, through the market as the buyers and sellers of commodities. The wool produced by the farmer is a commodity which he sells: it is bought by the spinner who sells it in turn, and so on down the line to the tailor. Thus, individual labour performed in isolation becomes part of a collective effort making work both individual and collective at the same time.

The chain that links the sheep-farmer, the spinner, the weaver and the tailor together is only one of many that exist in the economy. Moreover, these chains intersect with others to form a network or grid which embraces every individual producer in the society. Thus individuals, whose products are so remote from each other that their 'chains' do not intersect at all, are in close relation to each other as long as they are on this grid. The relationship, for example, between a tailor and a baker is, formally speaking, no different from that between the tailor and the weaver who makes the cloth for his coats, despite the fact that he does not use bread directly for his work. He relates to both as the buyer of their commodities, and can only do this because he has sold his commodity which may well have been bought by a carpenter, whose work makes no direct contribution to the making of either bread or coats. Every producer on the grid relates to every other producer, firstly through the matrix of productive interdependence, and secondly through the fact that any one individual can acquire the product of any other individual through exchange. The collectivity of labour in these circumstances is, therefore, not restricted to individuals who happen to be linked together on the same productive chain, it embraces all individuals in society. Under conditions of generalised commodity production individual labour, even where it is carried on in complete isolation, is a part of the collective labour of society, i.e. social labour.

These conditions, called *simple commodity production*, do not correspond directly to the full reality of capitalist society. Firstly, we are assuming that production occurs on a very small scale and that each producer works alone and relates to others exclusively as a buyer and seller of commodities. In capitalist society, production characteristically occurs on a large scale and workers are organised together in firms where their labour is directly co-ordinated. Secondly, every individual here is independent in the sense that no one is either an employer or an employee, and the only means of access to membership of the social labour force, or to what is the same thing, the acquisition of the products of social labour, is the performance of individual concrete labour. In capitalist society independence in this sense does not exist except for the tiny minority of self-employed people working alone and those who acquire money without having to work at all. On the other hand, all products in capitalist society take the form of commodities, with the result that the conditions of simple commodity production are unrealistic only in the sense of being incomplete. Although they do not describe the whole of capitalist society they do depict an aspect of it, and to the extent that capitalist society is a commodity-producing society, a fundamental aspect. The conclusions reached here, appropriately modified but not fundamentally changed, apply equally to the complex reality of capitalism.

What are these conclusions?

1. Corresponding to the two-fold nature of the commodity as a *use-*

value on the one side and an *exchange-value* on the other, labour also has a dual nature: as concrete labour it produces *use-value*, as abstract or social labour it produces value.

2. The abstract nature of labour is a social and not a physical characteristic; that is to say it is abstract labour only in so far as it counts as a part of the total labour of society, equivalent to, and no different from, any other type of labour.

3. Abstract labour is both the premise and the result of commodity exchange. If one type of concrete labour were not immanently the same as another, commodities could not be exchanged for each other on the basis of being the products of labour. This immanent identity of different types of labour is indicated by the mobility of labour from one task to another. But labour only really becomes abstract labour as a result of systematic exchange when the product of one type of labour is made equivalent to all others.

In the light of this, we need to change the proposition that a commodity has value because it is the product of labour, the magnitude of its value depending upon how much labour it embodies, to the following: a commodity has value because it is produced by *abstract* labour, and the amount of its value is determined by the amount of abstract labour that it requires under average conditions of production.

One last point needs to be made to link together value and money. We saw in the last section that money is the equivalent form of the labour-time embodied in a commodity, no matter how remote this might seem from daily experience. We now need to add that the labour-time that matters here is abstract labour-time: hence money is the equivalent form of the abstract labour embodied in a commodity; it is the *value-form* of the commodity. This value-form has, of course, physical independence of the commodity itself; it exists outside the commodity in the same way that pieces of iron exist outside the bread whose weight they represent. The internal division of the commodity into use-value on the one side and value on the other thus becomes externally and objectively expressed as a division between the world of commodities on the one side and money on the other. In this form it features in the daily experience of economic life. But it does this as something obvious and self-evident and it is impossible to tell from direct observation its true nature and implications. The division between commodities and money, between the natural form of commodities through which they serve as use-values, and their value-form, is a division of labour, a splitting of labour against itself, an alienation of labour which is the starting point of the mode of production that has capital at one pole and the working class at the other.

3 Surplus Value

We now have the theoretical elements we need, and the next task is to assemble them in the appropriate way. We begin with confrontation between commodities and money.

1. FROM SIMPLE CIRCULATION TO CAPITAL

Where C represents a commodity and M money, this confrontation takes two forms: $C - M$, a sale, and $M - C$, a purchase. These are the blocks with which the circulation of commodities is built and, combined, they give us the elementary form of that circulation, the *circuit of simple circulation*:

$$C - M - C'$$

A sale followed by a purchase: one commodity, C, is sold and with the proceeds another is bought, C'. (This second C is marked with a suffix (') to distinguish it from the first – a method of notation we employ from now on). This circuit is a monetised form of direct barter which resolves itself into an exchange of use-values where money plays a passive role. It is possible for one commodity to have a greater value than another but this is incidental to the circuit whose purpose is the exchange of use-values, and no changes in value are necessary for its movement. Suppose C is a coat made by a tailor in 10 hours with a monetary value of £10; and C' is 10 yards of linen which takes a weaver the same time to produce and has the same monetary value of £10: it follows that the tailor possesses a value of 10 hours at every point on the circuit. But the crucial point is that despite this constancy of value there is nevertheless a reason for exchange, namely the acquisition of a use-value that is wanted in return for one already possessed but not wanted. Variations in value can occur – the linen might have a value of 12 hours: but this is contingent to the exchange of use-values which is the impetus of simple circulation.

But the building blocks of circulation, $C - M$ and $M - C$ can be combined in the opposite way to produce a circuit where a different set of rules apply. This is:

$$M - C - M'$$

A purchase followed by a sale where only one commodity features and what is exchanged is one sum of money for another. No exchange makes sense unless its conclusion differs from its starting point; hence we suffix the second sum of money, M', to show that it is different from the first, M. But whereas the poles of the circuit of simple circulation are qualitatively different from each other, here the poles of the circuit are the same – both are money. The difference between them must, therefore, be quantitative. It is possible in some cases for M' to equal M; in others for M' to be less than M; but it is not possible to find the reason for the circuit in these terms, since the first result is a waste of time and the second a waste of money. The only rational explanation is that M' regularly exceeds M. As money is the form of existence of value, this positive difference between the second and the first sums of money amounts to a difference in value. In other words M' equals M *plus* an excess of value, or what is called *surplus value*.

Let us look at the differences between these two circuits in closer detail.

1. In the circuit $C - M - C'$ the movement of use value is primary and value plays a subordinate role. In the circuit $M - C - M'$ conditions are reversed and it is value that now takes the lead. Use-value represented by the commodity becomes merely the means of circulating value.

2. The circuit $C - M - C'$ retains a rational purpose even when all its elements have the same value, but this is not the case with $M - C - M'$ whose systematic repetition requires variations in value that lead to the regular accumulation of surplus value. Buying in order to sell can have no other purpose than *accumulation* which is by nature a continuous and endless process since the acquisition of one sum of money is only the point of departure for the acquisition of more. Hence the circuit, $M - C - M'$ defines a process of accumulation which resolves itself into a pursuit of pure quantity (wealth in the abstract) which can set no limits upon itself.

3. The circuit $C - M - C'$ is finite in the sense that it cannot immediately reproduce itself. Once the second commodity, C', is acquired it drops out of circulation and becomes an item of consumption. It is possible that an individual once having sold a commodity and bought another discovers a third which he would prefer, and sells the second to get it, thereby extending the circuit to $C - M - C' - M - C''$. And if he found a fourth commodity he wanted even more he could

make a further transaction and continue in this way to extend his circuit indefinitely. But these additional transactions only extend the existing circuit; sooner or later the acquired commodity is consumed and drops out of circulation. To start an entirely new circuit, a fresh commodity must be produced. Hence a string of these circuits is discontinuous:

$$C - M - C' : C - M - C' : C - M - C' :$$

The circuit $M - C - M'$, on the other hand, continuously renews itself since its terminal point, M', being money, is not immediately a use-value and lives its life perpetually in circulation. The end point of one circuit is the starting point for the next: hence we get a continuous chain:

$$M - C - M' - C - M'' - M''' - C - M''''$$

Moreover, this renewal takes place on an ever-expanding scale since each M is larger than the one preceding it; further indication of the purely quantitative nature of activity and the way in which the pursuit of surplus value posits endless accumulation.

These two circuits are the complete antithesis of each other, yet they comprise exactly the same elements – commodities and money; purchases and sales. Depending upon their arrangement the same elements give totally opposed results: $C - M - C'$, the circuit of simple circulation; and $M - C - M'$, which is the *general or characteristic form of the circuit of capital*. The important points can once again be enumerated for convenience.

1. The identical nature of the elements of the two circuits shows that capitalist circulation is only a special form of commodity circulation so that the concepts of value we have derived from conditions of simple commodity production are in general applicable to the more complex conditions of capitalism.

2. But if the elements of the circuit of capital are money and commodities, the same as the elements of simple circulation, capital becomes somewhat elusive, and it is legitimate to ask what it is, since it cannot be money and commodities as such. The answer is that it is money and commodities, but only in so far as they exist in the definite relationship to each other given by the circuit $M - C - M'$. More precisely: capital is the circuit $M - C - M''$ itself, the circulation of value or money in pursuit of itself; and money and commodities are merely the forms, the definite shapes, it assumes temporarily in its movement. Capital is value-in-motion, value in search of itself as surplus value, taking the form of money at one moment and commodities at the next.

But when money and commodities act as the receptacles of capital, its temporary embodiments, they cease to be money as such, and simple commodities and become *money-as-capital* and *commodities-as-capital*. In this guise they acquire additional characteristics but retain all their former properties: hence the analysis of capital must be preceded by the analysis of commodities and money.

3. Since the only rational purpose of $M - C - M'$ is surplus value and accumulation, it follows that this purpose defines the nature of capital. Capital is not a thing but a process – the search for surplus value on an ever-expanding scale. It is the nature of capital to accumulate as it is the nature of fire to burn, and just as it is impossible for a fire to exist without burning so it is impossible for capital to exist without accumulation.

The next step is to note how these circuits already anticipate the class division of capitalist society. Nobody can take to market a commodity he does not already own, and those who enter the market with money must already be in possession of it. In other words, that section of society whose economic activity is described by the circuit $M - C - M'$ must have access to money independently of circulation, and such independent wealth, we have seen, is the privilege of only a small section of society which we can designate the *capitalist class*. What does the rest of society take to market? Since it is not money it must be commodities of one form or another and the circuit that describes their activity must take the form $C - M - C''$ as they enter the market as sellers and leave it as buyers. But what commodity do they sell? The only thing they have that is marketable – their capacity to work or *labour-power*! Thus their circuit takes the form $L - M - C'$, where L represents labour-power, M, the money they receive for it (the wage) and C', the commodities they buy. This circuit of labour visibly shares the general characteristics of simple circulation, starting and ending with commodities, a sale followed by a purchase: hence it is the complete antithesis of the circuit of capital. Where the working class enters economic life with one use-value in search of another, the capitalist class enters it with value in search of more value – surplus value.

It is no argument against this to say that some workers are interested only in money and many capitalists appreciate the better things in life, since here we are only concerned with workers and capitalists as the representatives of their class, with *workers-in-general* and *capitalists-in-general*. Whatever the individual aspirations a person might have in so far as he is a worker he sells in order to buy, and in so far as he is a capitalist he buys in order to sell. As these two activities are the polar opposites of each other, so the worker and the capitalist are worlds apart.

2. SURPLUS VALUE

Surplus value is a composite of *surplus* and *value* indicating that on the one hand it originates in the difference between total production and the consumption necessary to sustain it, and on the other that it is the product of abstract labour. But this is not apparent in the general form of the circuit of capital, $M - C - M'$ where it appears as the simple result of exchange lending support to the popular myth that profit, the guise in which surplus value is commonly known, is due simply to buying cheap and selling dear. Although it is only fair to point out that this elementary tautology, which comprises the worldly wisdom of every small businessman and backstreet cheat, has never found a place in the canons of economic orthodoxy, it is worth brief consideration since its refutation provides a useful starting point from which to discover the source of surplus value.

In so far as the circuit of capital opens with a purchase and closes with a sale, no surplus value or profit can accrue unless the price of the sale is greater than that of the purchase. But this inequality of exchange is only the medium through which profits are *realised*: by analogy, throwing a switch to put on a light realises electricity but does not generate it, and any investigation into the nature of electricity which restricted itself to the examination of switches would reveal very little. Imagine a group of businessmen trading together, each one in search of profit. Firstly, it is clear that the profits of this intra-group trade must work out at zero since gains on one side are matched by compensating losses on the other. Secondly, if the group trades with another group its members can acquire a positive net profit; but the second group, in so far as it is distinct from the first rather than a mere extension of it, must engage in economic activities other than buying and selling, and these other activities must be the real source of the positive net profit, since trading, as we have just seen, creates no net profit at all. We will examine the precise economic functions of exchange in detail in Chapter 7.3. For the moment, it is enough to confirm that buying and selling can alter the profitability of individual firms – individual *capitals* as we can call them – but cannot affect total profits – the profits of *total* or *social capital*—one way or another.

This point must be stressed: the analysis of surplus value or profit must start at the level of social capital and not with the individual firm where anything is possible. When we ask the question in these terms—what is the source of total surplus value?—only one answer is possible:

production! There are many ways of seeing why this must be so, but the most straightforward is this: surplus value appears in the first place as a sum of money, but is acceptable in this form only because it can be used to purchase commodities. Hence the realisation of surplus value through buying and selling requires the production of surplus commodities if it is to be anything more than a symbolic act: buying cheap and selling dear is only the outer and visible aspect of surplus production. To express the same point theoretically it is only necessary to recall that money through which surplus value first appears is nothing but the value form of commodities and the only way commodities can acquire value is through the application of labour in the process of production.

To accommodate this conclusion we must modify the circuit of capital which in its general form $M - C - M'$ makes no mention of the activity that gives it substance. In its place we must put the *circuit of industrial capital*:

$$M - C^L_{MP} \ldots P \ldots C' \ldots M'$$

where M and C retain their meaning as do the suffixes ($'$); L, represents labour-power; MP, the means of production; and P, production. As a formal description of capitalist enterprise this circuit is straightforward: money capital is used to hire workers and buy means of production, $M - C^L_{MP}$, which are then organised in the process of production, P, whose result is the output of commodities different from those originally purchased, C'. The circuit concludes with a sale that returns capital to its original money form, $C' - M'$, where it is in a position to renew itself.

Industrial, here, does not mean manufacturing industry: it applies equally well to agriculture. The circuit is called the circuit of industrial capital because it includes the process of production in its movement. In this respect it is different from the general form of the circuit of capital, $M - C - M$, but it shares the fundamental feature of this circuit, beginning and ending with money and having the pursuit of surplus value as its exclusive purpose.

As we examine it in detail we see that it comprises two sets of apparently unrelated changes; the transformation of C^L_{MP} into C' and of M into M'. In the case of a car factory C^L_{MP} comprises the labour-power of the different types of workers employed plus the machinery, tools and materials that production requires; while C' represents cars. Only production can bring about the transformation from one to the other: this transformation is, after all, the definition of production. But at the same time as it brings about the change of C^L_{MP} into C', the process of production is responsible for the change of M into M' – surplus value. As

Surplus Value

the sphere of two simultaneously changes – one in material substance, the other in value – it follows that the process of production in capitalist society has a dual character. This corresponds to the dual character of its result – the commodity – which is a use-value and a value at one and the same time. On the one side there is material production (use-value) and on the other value production (value and surplus value). In the next chapter we will see how these two aspects of production combine and condition each other but here we are concerned with its value aspect alone.

Consider a car factory by way of illustration, bearing in mind that we are interested in the production of cars only in so far as it is capitalist production, and in the economics of an individual capital only in so far as it is representative of general or social capital. Suppose this factory turns out 6,000 cars each year, which requires 6 million hours of labour, half living labour and half dead labour in the form of the means of production. (For convenience we also assume that the means of production are entirely used up within the year; that the machines work effectively until the final car is ready and then become completely useless. This is not entirely plausible but it simplifies the analysis without affecting its conclusions.)

If now we suppose that every hour of labour, both living and dead, can be represented as £1, the value of car production can be depicted as follows:

value derived from means of production requiring 3 million hours of labour	£3.0 million
new value added by 3 million hours of labour	£3.0 million
value of 6,000 cars	£6.0 million

Supposing the means of production consists of two parts – one part machinery and the other materials – this schema is easily modified:

value derived from machinery (2 million hours)	£2.0 million
value derived from materials (1 million hours)	£1.0 million
new value added by 3 million hours of living labour	£3.0 million
value of 6,000 cars	£6.0 million

So much is clear: but is it legitimate to represent an hour of labour by the same amount of money, here £1, irrespective of its form (living or dead) and by implication assume what is called *equal* or *equivalent exchange*? It is not the particular sum of £1 that is called into question – we could equally have £10 or 10 pence; but the fixed ratio of money-price to labour time – i.e. machinery, £2 million:2 million hours; materials,

£1 million:1million hours; cars, £6 million:6 million hours. Is it legitimate to adopt a system of representing value in money terms which implies that the prices of commodities are proportionate to their values? The answer is that this procedure is not only legitimate in the present circumstances, but mandatory. Remember we are not concerned with individual commodities and firms except in so far as they are representative of total output and social capital, and at this level net surplus value cannot be created by exchange. The only effective means of keeping exchange clear of the analysis of surplus value is to assume that every commodity is bought and sold at a price proportionate to its value, thereby imposing on the individual firm the conditions that apply to social capital which makes no surplus value through trade. In this respect equal exchange far from being an illicit assumption smuggled in to explain surplus value is a rigorous condition on which it is to be explained.

In fact it is such a rigorous condition that it appears to make surplus value totally impossible. The cars sell for £6 million: the capitalist has to pay £3 million for his means of production and apparently a further £3 million as wages, since we must assume that equal exchange covers all commodities, including those sold by workers. If the money price of 3 million hours of dead labour is £3 million, the price of 3 million hours of living labour must be the same. But if it is, where can the firm get surplus value for its outlays equal to its receipts? Equal exchange not only disqualifies exchange as a source of surplus value but also the means of production. These comprise half the value of the cars (3 million) but the capitalist has spent this amount to get them. Only living labour is left, but this appears no more promising since the conditions of equal exchange apparently demand that the capitalist must pay £3 million as wages for the 3 million hours of living labour he acquires from his employees. *Hic Rhodos, hic salta!*

3. LABOUR AND LABOUR-POWER

The problem then is this: every source of surplus value except living labour is disqualified, but living labour is apparently disqualified on the same grounds. In the course of a year the workers produce a value of 3 million hours and on the face of it there seems no reason, given the condition of equal exchange, why they should not receive £3 million in return. But if they do, the capitalist who has already advanced £3 million against his means of production has a total outlay equal to his receipts,

Surplus Value

£6 million, hence no surplus value. But here as elsewhere appearances are deceptive; in fact, the wage contract, which is what concerns us here, is one of the most illusory of all economic phenomena and requires the closest examination. Part of this we must do right away and then go over the question even more thoroughly in Chapter 6.

The issue revolves around exactly what it is the worker sells to the capitalist. What exactly does the capitalist buy from the worker in return for the wage he pays? The obvious answer, *labour*, will not do: this is what the capitalist gets not what he buys. The matter is less confusing than it appears.

Consider a commodity that is bought and sold – a car, a coat or whatever. The reason for purchasing any commodity, except where the buyer is a capitalist interested in its immediate resale, is the use to be derived from it – transport in the case of the car, warmth in the case of the coat, and so on. But the customer does not purchase these things directly; he does not actually buy transport and warmth, but physical objects, use-values, which yield these services only after they are bought and put to use. When he buys a car we can say he buys potential transport; a coat, potential warmth; food, potential nourishment and so on. Or to look at it from the other side, transport is the realised use of a car; warmth, the realised use of a coat and so on. In this light we can pose the question again, what is it that the capitalist buys from the worker, and get a significant answer that breaks the deadlock. Whatever it is, its realised use is 3 million hours of labour. But what he actually buys is as different from 3 million hours of labour as a car is from 50,000 miles of transport. He buys a use-value whose potential is 3 million hours of labour; in other words he buys the potential of labour or as it is commonly called the capacity to labour or *labour-power*.

Let us suppose that the 3 million hours are supplied by 1,500 men who work a 40 hour week for 50 weeks a year. What, in these circumstances, is labour-power? And what is its value?

The ability or capacity to work is above all a human attribute, so that the presence of labour-power as a commodity that capitalists can buy requires human beings fit and healthy enough to work. In this case it requires 1,500 of them who must be kept capable of work throughout the whole year. But this is not all: when we look at capitalist production as a whole, and remember that it continues from one year to the next, it is clear that the working class must be reproduced continuously. This involves sustaining not only those currently at work but making provision for the next generation, the retired and those unable to work for one reason or another. In other words, the continuous availability of labour-power as a commodity requires the reproduction of the working class, and this can only happen if the class gains access to a part of the social product for purposes of *necessary personal consumption*—food, clothing, housing etc. Much dispute surrounds the question of what items should be considered necessary in this context; whether such things as cars and television sets should be included under this head, or whether it should be restricted to the basic essentials only. We shall take this matter up in Chapter 6: for the moment it is only necessary to remember that the items of necessary consumption in capitalist society, however broadly or narrowly we define 'necessary' in this context, are commodities that can only be acquired with money. Thus the continuous availability of labour-power as a commodity for capitalists to buy, requires in its turn the continuous availability to the working class of sufficient amounts of money for it to purchase items of necessary consumption.

Let us translate this proposition into value terms. Labour-power, in so far as it is a commodity, is a use-value like other commodities and also an embodiment of value. In both respects it has important peculiarities. Its use-value is unique in that it realises itself as labour that produces value. As value, it is also unlike all other commodities in so far as it is not directly produced by wage-labour. The labour that is necessary for the production of labour-power does not produce it directly, but the commodities necessary to sustain the workers; that is to say it produces labour-power indirectly. (It is true that a certain amount of labour is engaged directly in the production of labour-power, notably housework which is almost invariably done by women, but this is not wage-labour paid directly by capital and provision for the necessary consumption of housewives is included in the husband's wage.) In determining the value of labour-power the capitalist economy takes account only of the labour that produces those commodities which form the necessary consumption of the working class, and it is the value of these commodities that constitutes the value of labour-power. We need to add that each individual capitalist contributes to this amount in proportion to the number of workers he employs, directly through the payment of wages, and indirectly through taxes and insurance that are used to provide such public services as health and education that are necessary for the reproduction of labour-power, and pensions and social security payments for those that do not work.

There are, then, surrounding labour-power two distinct magnitudes of value. On the one side is the value derived from its use or consumption, the value produced by the labour realised from the labour-power. In our example this amounts to 3 million hours, or £3 million, locked up in commodities, cars, which are the property of the capitalist. On the other side is the value of labour-power itself, the value of the commodities necessary to sustain the workers who supply the labour-power. This is the value of the commodity that the worker sells to the capitalist and therefore the value that the capitalist has to pay when he hires workers. The commonly used term, the *value of labour*, obliterates this distinction: if an hour of labour is the substance of value, then what is the value of x hours of labour but x hours of labour? Or of 3 million hours of labour but 3 million hours of labour? It is the implication of this expression that creates the apparently insurmountable problem of discovering how living labour can be the source of surplus value after all other possible sources have been disqualified. But once we appreciate the distinction between labour-power and labour and understand that there is not one magnitude of value involved but two – the value of labour-power and the value produced by the labour derived from this labour-power – we can begin to see daylight.

It is, of course, possible that these two amounts of value, although distinct from each other, could actually be equal. This would be the case in our example if the commodities that made up the annual diet of necessary consumption for the 1,500 workers required 3 million hours to produce. In these conditions the capitalist would indeed make no surplus value, for the value of the labour-power he purchases would equal the 3 million hours of labour that the workers put into his commodities. But though such equality is possible it is by no means necessary or inevitable. The fact that a man works eight hours a day does not mean that the products required to sustain him to do this work should take the same time to produce. If this were the case, mankind could never have developed beyond the level of bare subsistence. It could be argued that morally a man is entitled to consume the equivalent of what he produces, but this is quite beside the point here, where we are only concerned with what he needs to consume in order to produce, and from the dawn of history men have always produced more than they needed in this sense. They have, in a word, always achieved a surplus production. By the time capitalist society emerged some two hundred years ago this had already reached considerable proportions.

But how do capitalists gain control of this surplus? How does surplus production become surplus value?

To postulate surplus production as a structural feature of capitalist society is to say the value produced by labour is greater than the value of the labour-power that yields that labour. The annual product of society represents in a physical form a definite expenditure of labour, part of which is contributed by dead labour in the form of means of production and the other part by living labour. The depreciation of the means of production equals the value they contribute to the new product so this item nets out. We are left with the contribution made by living labour and where surplus production occurs this amount is more than sufficient to meet the necessary consumption of the workers. In other words, the living workers produce each year a value in excess of what is needed to maintain them: they produce a value in excess of the value of their labour-power.

Returning to the example, let us assume that the commodities needed by the 1,500 workers during the course of the year take 1.5 million hours to produce. The figure is arbitrary and chosen only for arithmetic convenience. The value of labour-power, the value, that is, of the commodity which the workers sell to the capitalist, equals this amount. Thus assuming equal exchange and the ratio of £1 to one hour of labour, the capitalist pays his workers £1.5 million in wages during the course of the year. But these workers do 3 million hours labour in the twelve months and, therefore, add a value of £3 million to commodities that are the property of the capitalist. When the capitalist sells his stock at the end of the year, he pockets the difference, £1.5 million, and calls it profit. This gives him a healthy balance sheet:

	£ million
value derived from the means of production	3.0
value added by living labour	3.0
value of 6,000 cars	6.0
less	
cost of means of production/depreciation	3.0
value of labour-power/wages	1.5
surplus value/profit	1.5

Of course balance sheets do not actually look like this since it would give the whole game away: first, that profit is surplus value; and second, that surplus value is the difference between what workers produce and what they are paid. But whatever the system of account this is the reality they present – or to be accurate, misrepresent.

It can be easily seen that the way this £1.5 million surplus value is acquired satisfies all the conditions set down earlier. None of it comes by buying cheap and selling dear, since every commodity exchanges at value. The final output, the cars, sell for £6 million and the capitalist purchases at value all the commodities he needs to undertake their production. At the same time no profit is made from the means of production: they add £3 million to the value of the cars on the one hand but costs the capitalist £3 million on the other. Profit consists entirely of surplus value, the difference between the new value created by labour and the value of the necessary commodities consumed by the workers. This represents the value of the labour-power the workers sell, and the value the capitalist pays them in wages. In short, the capitalist pays his workers the full value of their labour-power and makes his profit without recourse to sharp practices, cheating or magic.

4. THE LEGITIMACY OF EXPLOITATION

Where labour-power is exchanged for value, the whole of the surplus product of society takes the form of surplus value and is appropriated by capital as profit. But this raises a fine question: can we legitimately assume equal exchange here for the conditions that applied where we made the assumption earlier, no longer apply? Critics of the theory of surplus value have long maintained that it rests upon an arbitrary assertion of equal exchange, and it is extremely important that we get the matter clear and see exactly what is the connection between surplus value and equal exchange.

First, we must acknowledge that the implications of exchange between capital and labour are not the same as those of exchange among capitalists: unlike intra-capitalist trade, exchange between labour and capital can affect the total size of surplus value. In our example surplus value equals £1.5 million when we assume that capital buys labour-power at its value; but if it buys it above value, at say £2 million, surplus value falls accordingly to £1 million. (Remember this example concerns a representative firm and that all the conclusions we draw from it apply to social capital.) The grounds on which we dismissed deviation between value and price do not apply to labour-power and at the same time deviations with respect to labour-power have much greater significance than they have for other commodities. Thus the critic of the theory of surplus value is apparently on strong ground here: remove the condition that all commodities must exchange at their values, he can argue, and the theory of surplus value loses its cutting edge. There is no longer any reason why it should equal total surplus production, no reason, even, for it to have a positive magnitude at all, since it is possible in principle for the workers to bid up the wage rate to a level where profits are zero.

But even if we were to grant the whole of this criticism we would concede nothing of importance. The conditions concerning exchange among capitalists remain intact and net profit can never be acquired here. If capitalist A buys his means of production below their value from capitalist B he only gains at the latter's expense; while the ulterior suggestion that profit can be derived from the use of machinery contravenes the most elementary law of economics that new or net production can only be achieved by human labour acting upon nature. At the same time the fact that the amount of surplus value is no longer determinate and that, in principle, profits would fall to zero if wages rose above the value of labour-power, only reinforces the main tenet of the theory of surplus value, that it comprises unpaid labour, the difference between what workers produce and what they are paid.

It would, however, weaken the theory considerably if the equal exchange of labour-power were to be forced out, since it would be left without any quantitative determination. There are compelling reasons for retaining it, though not the ones we might expect. It appears that the equal exchange of labour-power is the premise from which the existence and the scale of surplus value are derived; but in reality the reverse applies, and it is the nature of surplus value that is the premise and the tendency of wages to equal the value of labour-power that is the consequence. This might appear a precious point of theory, but it is crucial to the dynamics of the capitalist economy and its recurrent lurches into crises of depression.

At the beginning of this chapter we saw that capital arises out of the double nature of the commodity and its development into the separation of commodities on the one hand, from money, on the other. This separation give us first the circuit of simple circulation, $C - M - C'$, but the elements out of which this circuit is built, $C - M$, a purchase, and $M - C$, a scale, give us $M - C - M'$, the circuit of capital and surplus value. In other words, surplus value is logically prior, as it was indeed historically prior, to the buying and selling of labour-power as a commodity and the whole question of the rate at which it is exchanged. Equally we saw that surplus value, in so far as it is its own reason, is nothing but the pursuit of pure quantity, with the result that once the circuit of capital has established itself the question is not simply a search for surplus value, but for *maximum* surplus value. It is true that capitalists often adopt a long-term perspective and sacrifice short-term gains for greater profits in the long run, but this changes nothing substantial. The impetus of capital to acquire surplus value is, by definition, an impetus to

Surplus Value

acquire the greatest amount of surplus value possible. But when capital has developed into its full industrial form where it controls the productive process and hires labour directly, the maximum amount of surplus value consistent with the reproduction of society occurs when the share of the working class in the social product is reduced to its absolute minimum, that is, when workers are paid the value of their labour-power. In other words, it is the process of capitalist production itself and the pursuit of surplus value that brings about the equal exchange of labour-power, not vice versa.

At the same time, the power of the working class to resist this tendency must not be ignored, and it is possible, both in principle and in practice, for determined action on its part, particularly in times of boom, to force wages up above the value of labour-power and reduce surplus value proportionately. But in doing this, it must be stressed, it places itself in opposition not just to a group of individual capitalists driven by greed to get as much as they can, but to the very nature of capital itself and the whole system of capitalist production. In other words, any successful drive by the working class that pushes wages above the value of labour-power calls forth a systemic response that is extremely complicated in its articulation and often confusing in the particular tactical goals it seeks to achieve, but has always only one real end in view – the re-establishment of the wage rate at a level equivalent to the value of labour-power. Thus what appears at first sight to be a simple technical assumption and a remote issue of theory turns out to be the key strategic point of class relationship in capitalist society. This is another question taken up in some detail in Chapter 6.

One final point on surplus value and the equal exchange of labour-power needs to be made at this stage. It is easy to gain the impression that equal exchange is a simplifying assumption to make the explanation of surplus value easy, whereas the contrary is the case. If we drop the assumption, we open the possibility for capital to pay workers less than the value of their labour-power and to profit at their expense by cheating. But if capital is forced to trade at value it gains nothing by unfair practice. The terms on which it deals with workers are exactly the same as those on which individual capitalist, deal with each other. In terms of market legality, whereby everyone should be paid the equivalent of what he sells, the worker has no cause for complaint when a capitalist pays him the value of his labour-power. But even under these conditions he is paid for only a portion of the labour he performs – the part that is equivalent of the value of his labour-power – while the capitalist appropriates the other portion for nothing. In a word the worker is *exploited*; exploitation and the production of surplus value being one and the same thing – the performance of unpaid labour. But this exploitation, it must be stressed, is not the result of sharp practice and is therefore not accessible to change by legal reform. Quite the opposite: in so far as legality involves fair contract, and upholding the law means that everyone, capitalists and workers alike, can rightfully claim an equivalent payment for his commodity, to this extent the law enshrines and reinforces exploitation.

5. FORMAL DEFINITIONS

This is a convenient time to pause and work briefly through the various terms and forms of notation in which the theory of surplus value is conventionally expressed.

At the start of the circuit money capital is advanced against the means of of production and labour-power, $M - C^L_{MP}$ as capital divides itself up into different forms corresponding to the various elements of production. That part of capital advanced against the means of production is commonly called *constant capital*, the term reflecting the facts that first it is capital, and second, that it is capital advanced in such a way that its value does not change in the course of the circuit. Our 'balance sheet' on p. 38 shows that the value entered against the means of production is the same above and below the line – i.e. the value the means of production cost at the start of the circuit is the same as their contribution to the value of the product at the end. The second element of capital, that advanced against labour-power is known as *variable capital* and the same logic applies. First it is a form of capital, but second, this element of capital has a changing value, since the value paid for labour-power at the beginning of the circuit does not equal the value contributed to the product by living labour.

Translating the circuit of capital into these terms is a straightforward job:

$$M = MP + L \qquad (1)$$
$$= c + v \qquad (2)$$

where c represents constant capital; and v variable capital. Thus

$$M' = c + v + s \qquad (3)$$

where s represents surplus value,
and

$$M' - M = s \qquad (4)$$

Surplus Value

These three elements – constant capital, c, variable capital, v, and surplus value, s, embody the theory as we have developed it so far. From now on we will be concerned with their mutual actions upon each other as expressed through three critical ratios which we define here as a point of reference.

1. $\dfrac{s}{v}$ — *the rate of surplus value*
2. $\dfrac{s}{c+v}$ — *the rate of profit*
3. $\dfrac{c}{v}$ — *the organic composition of capital.*

4 Absolute and Relative Surplus Value

The first of these ratios, the *rate of surplus value*, is the most crucial, since it is the one that directly summarises the economic relations between the class antagonists of capitalist society. If we add together surplus value and variable capital for a society for the period of, say a year, we get the annual total of *new* production. New production is total production less the amount needed to replace used up means of production – what is conventionally called net national income. The ratio of surplus value to variable capital is therefore, first of all, a measure of income distribution between the capitalist class on the one side, and the working class on the other. But new value is entirely the product of living labour which receives only a proportion of it back as wages. Thus the rate of surplus value is an indicator of exploitation as well as income distribution, measuring the ratio of paid to unpaid labour performed by the working class.

We have seen that the search for surplus value arises from the nature of capital itself as a movement of value, $M - C - M'$ and that this inevitably means the pursuit of maximum surplus value. Clearly the absolute amount of surplus value that capital can acquire is a vital indicator of its success, but an incomplete one. Two different capitals may both acquire a surplus value of £1 million but if one has advanced £1 million and the other £2 million in its acquisition, it is clear that the first capital is more successful that the second – in this case twice as successful. In other words, the criterion that matters for capital is not the absolute amount of surplus value taken in isolation, but in relation to the amount advanced to procure it. So much is obvious but there is a slight complication which we must clear away before going on.

The ratio that concerns the practical capitalist is that of surplus value to the total capital advanced in obtaining it, that is the rate of profit not the rate of surplus value. In making his calculations the capitalist reckons that he advances one sum of money, M, and recovers a second sum, M', and what counts for him is the difference between these two sums in relation to the first – i.e. $\dfrac{M'-M}{M}$. But we know (from p. 42 above):

$$M' = c + v + s$$

and

$$M = c + v$$

therefore

$$\frac{M'-M}{M} = \frac{(c+v+s)-(c+v)}{c+v}$$

$$P' = \frac{s}{c+v} = \text{the rate of profit}$$

If we take this last expression and divide all its elements by v we get the following alternative expression of the rate of profit:

$$\frac{s}{c+v} = \frac{s}{v} \div \left(1 + \frac{c}{v}\right)$$

From this we can see that the rate of profit is a ratio of two ratios; the rate of surplus value and the organic composition of capital. When we study the rate of profit in Chapter 7 we will examine the organic composition of capital closely, but in this chapter we will proceed as though the rate of surplus value and the rate of profit were identical. This makes exposition easier and does not invalidate any conclusions since whatever happens to the organic composition of capital, the fact remains that any increase in the rate of surplus value tends to increase the rate of profit. In its pursuit of maximum profit capital must maximise the rate of surplus value, that is the rate at which it exploits labour – even if it is not fully conscious of the fact.

1. ABSOLUTE SURPLUS VALUE

In what follows we are concerned exclusively with the *rate* of surplus value, and when we talk of *absolute surplus value* we mean a particular aspect of the rate of surplus value and not the absolute amount of surplus value referred to a moment ago.

We know that the total new value produced in an economy is the sum of surplus value and the value paid to the workers as variable capital. In other words, it is the product of a definite amount of labour time expended by living workers. One fraction of this time is spent producing the equivalent of the workers' needs – the value of labour-power. This part is called *necessary labour time* since its product serves the needs of necessary consumption as defined by the requirement of basic reproduction considered in Chapter 2. The personal consumption of the producers – in capitalist society, the working class – is an essential condition for maintaining production, and in this sense necessary. The other part is called *surplus labour time*.

We can apply this distinction to the working day by means of a simple illustration. Let us represent the length of the working day as a line AB, and on this line have a point C, so that AC represents the necessary part of the working day during which the worker reproduces the equivalent of his labour-power, and CB the surplus part when he produces surplus value for capital. AC, in other words, represents the paid part of the working day and BC the unpaid part.
Thus:

$$A \text{————} C \text{————} B$$

If the working day lasts 8 hours, AB = 8. If it takes the worker 4 hours to produce the equivalent of his labour-power, then both necessary labour-time, AC, and surplus labour-time, CB = 4, and the rate of surplus value equals 100 per cent, i.e. CB:AC. It is this ratio that capital strives to maximise.

Let us suppose AC is fixed and nothing can be done to reduce it. Working class consumption is already at a minimum and there are no techniques at hand to economise labour in its production. In these circumstances the only way to increase the rate of surplus value is to extend CB by lengthening the working day.

$$A \text{————} C \text{————} B \text{————} B' \text{————} B''$$

Where AC equals 4 hours and the length of the working day is 8 hours, CB also equals 4 hours and the rate of surplus value equals 100 per cent. If the working day is increased to 12 hours, AB′, with AC unchanged at 4 hours, the surplus part of the working day rises to 8 hours, CB′, and the rate of surplus value grows proportionately to 200 per cent. A further increase in the working day to 16 hours, AB″, under the same conditions causes it to rise to 300 per cent. This method of increasing the rate of surplus value by extending the length of the working day on the basis of a fixed and low wage is called the *production of absolute surplus value*.

It is possible, of course, that the lengthening of working hours will require an increase in wages simply to support the additional effort. But

Absolute and Relative Surplus Value

this is not the major limitation inherent in this mode of exploitation – an increase in AC by say one hour is still profitable to capital if it can increase CB by a greater amount. There is little evidence to suggest that in Britain in the early nineteenth century, where the production of absolute surplus value was the order of the day, capital had to concede any wage increases on this count. All types of union activity were severely repressed, and the workers who performed 18 hours a day and above, usually earned wages barely sufficient to cover their most basic needs. The most important shortcoming of this strategy for capital is to be found elsewhere in the definite limits it places on growth. Given the fact that the working day has natural limits, the pace of accumulation must slow down once the whole available population has been dragged into the proletariat.

But even before this occurs other pressures begin to assert themselves. It is one thing to make a worker do a 16 hour day, it is quite another to maintain the intensity of work for that time, though history records many successful attempts to achieve this, ranging from harsh discipline to handcuffing the worker to the machine. But it is a general rule that long hours worked continuously day after day reduce the effectiveness of work, and there are few workers who do as much in the 14th hour of a day as in the 4th. Each additional hour the worker is kept beyond the threshold of, say 8, adds progressively less to the total amount of work done. Though in formal terms the capitalist might acquire 12 hours of labour time from a 16 hour day, he might, in practice, find that the product of these 12 hours equals the product of only 6 hours of a fresh worker. But this is not all. The wear and tear of low wages and long hours takes its toll on workers, and it is not only the amount of work done in the closing hours of the day that tends to fall, but that done in the early part as well. To maintain the rate of surplus value – to the capitalist this will appear as maintaining the level of efficiency in his factory – fresh workers have to be drafted in as old ones are exhausted, and this begins to tilt the labour market in favour of workers who can start to bid for higher wages. At the same time the need for ever harsher discipline and supervision in the factory grows, all of which involves the capitalist in extra costs. One way and another, the production of absolute surplus value suffers the most definite drawbacks as a strategy of long term accumulation, as British capital, which climbed to world dominance through its deployment, began to learn by the middle of the nineteenth century. The struggle for the ten hour day by the working class drove this lesson home, and by 1850 the economies to be reaped from higher wages and shorter working days began to dawn upon Britain's leading capitalists. Gradually the mode of exploitation changed towards the production of relative surplus value.

2. RELATIVE SURPLUS VALUE

Let us suppose the length of the working day, AB, is fixed at, say 8 hours. In this case the only way of increasing the rate of surplus value is to shorten necessary working time and reduce AC.

A————————C————————B

If the necessary part of the working day is 4 hours, the rate of surplus value we have seen is 100 per cent: if AC is reduced to say 2 hours and CB correspondingly increased to 6 hours, the rate of surplus value rises to 300 per cent. In contradistinction to increases in the rate of surplus value achieved by extending the working day (the production of absolute surplus value), increases brought about by reducing necessary labour time are called the production of *relative surplus value*. The simple arithmetic of this operation conceals two important features of the economic processes involved and we must give these our close attention.

1. The only way in which the necessary part of the working day can be reduced – i.e. the value of labour-power lowered systematically and permanently – is by an increase in the productivity of labour employed in the wage-goods sector of the economy. The necessary consumption of the working class is first of all a definite mass of use-values, so much food, clothing etc. Assume the basket of goods to be a fixed amount: it follows then, that variations in the value of labour-power occur solely as a result of changes in the amount of labour necessary to produce this basket. If improved techniques of production halve the amount of labour required, the value of labour-power is cut in two; although the real wage and the working-class living standards are unaffected. In other words, improvements in productivity which reduce the value of wage-goods, reduce the necessary part of the working day; therefore increase the surplus part and allow the rate of surplus value to go up without any reduction in real wages.

This is not all. Take the initial situation where half the working day is made up of necessary labour and the other half of surplus labour giving a rate of surplus value of 100 per cent. Assume once again a doubling of productivity in the wage-goods sector that allows the existing level of real wages to be produced in half the time, but now suppose that the working class reacts to the increase in capitalist profitability and successfully struggles for a rise of 50 per cent in real wages. They increase the basket of use-values they can buy by one half. The following table illustrates what happens:

	Initial situation	Productivity doubled in wage-goods sector
real wage (index)	100	150
value of wage (hours)	4	3
surplus labour (hours)	4	5
rate of surplus value	100 %	166 %

The production of this larger real wage would require 6 hours at the original level of productivity: but productivity has doubled so it only requires 3 hours. AC is therefore reduced to 3, and the surplus part of the working day, CB, goes up to 5 hours, giving a rate of surplus value of 166 per cent. In other words, with the production of relative surplus value, it is not only possible for the rate of surplus value to go up without any fall in the level of real wages, but for it to go up while real wages are themselves rising. This apparently paradoxical result that the exploitation of labour does not inevitably lead to a reduction in working class living standards, that on the contrary, exploitation and living standards can rise together, is not a theoretical anomaly but a general statement of one of the fundamental relations of the capitalist political economy. First, it makes clear how working class 'affluence' is possible within the framework of the capitalist economy, and at the same time, explains why the advent of 'affluence' does not in itself change the class relations of exploitation that are characteristic of capitalism. Second, the production of relative surplus value is the result of improvements in productivity; and this explains why the continuous search for new techniques that constantly revolutionise the process of production must be placed alongside the continuous impulse to accumulate as a permanent feature of capitalist society.

2. The reduction in the value of labour-power upon which the production of relative surplus value rests cannot be achieved by individual firms but only by their collective action, and is, therefore, a mode of exploitation that rests upon social capital as such. With the production of absolute surplus value, an individual capital can increase its own rate of surplus value by extending the working day of its employees, and although firms always benefit directly from their own actions, the main advantages accruing from the production of relative surplus value are achieved indirectly by collective action. The wage-

goods that form the necessary consumption of the workers are produced by a wide range of industries involving many different firms, even today when the size of firms relative to output is much greater than ever before. A single firm produces only a small portion of the commodities the working class consumes, and because of the high degree of specialisation, its output satisfies only a small fraction of the needs of its own workers. Hence an increase in productivity that is restricted to a single enterprise, although it increases the profitability of that enterprise, has a negligible effect upon the value of labour-power and therefore makes an insignificant contribution to the production of relative surplus value by itself. Only a general increase in productivity in the production of the wage-goods sector can lower the value of labour-power and increase relative surplus value.

The social dimension of this mode of exploitation is further illustrated by the fact that even those firms that do not produce wage-goods also benefit to the extent that the reduction in the value of labour lowers the amount of variable capital they need to advance. It would be incorrect to conclude that this social interdependence of capital only began when the production of relative surplus became the order of the day, and that it was unknown when the production of absolute surplus value prevailed. But it is vastly more important when the production of relative surplus value is the main mode of exploitation, since the success or failure of the individual capitalist enterprise becomes increasingly dependent upon the success or failure of social capital as a whole. The fact that individual capitalists may be unaware of this, and hold on to a philosophy and practice of competition that lays all the onus on individual enterprise, is besides the point. Here, as elsewhere, everything appears to be the opposite of what it really is, and the competition among capitalists and their mutual opposition to each other, is nothing more than the curious manner in which they unite together to form a regular masonic society in the face of the working class upon whose exploitation they all depend.

Modern capitalism, especially in its advanced metropolitan centres, is now almost exclusively dependent upon the production of relative surplus value and these two aspects of its operation – the continuous tendency for the productivity of labour to increase and the social interdependence of capital – form the central themes of most of what follows.

3. THE MODES COMBINED

In theoretical terms the distinction between absolute and relative surplus value is clear-cut. In one case the value of labour-power remains constant at a level that gives the worker a miserable standard of living, and surplus value is increased by extending the working day; in the other, surplus value is increased by reductions in the value of labour-power while the length of the working day is held constant. In practice the distinction is more blurred and at any moment considerable variations exist among different countries and different industries. For instance, in the second half of the nineteenth century the production of relative surplus value was more advanced in the United States than it was in Britain; while in Britain itself, it was more advanced in the engineering industry than it was in the coal or textile industries. Nevertheless, we can validly use the production of absolute and relative surplus value as the criterion for defining phases of capitalist development; in fact there is no more important criterion for this purpose than the *characteristic mode of exploitation*. Dating is inevitably imprecise, though few authorities would disagree that the production of absolute surplus value was the dominant mode of exploitation before 1850 and the production of relative surplus value after 1950. Beyond this, consensus is difficult; but this is significant in itself, for the fact that the transition from one mode to another could have taken as long as a century is indicative of both its scope and its scale. It is one thing to distinguish absolute surplus value from relative surplus value in theory, it is quite a different thing to execute a transition from one to the other in practice.

First there is the development and application of the new techniques necessary to increase the productivity of labour. Although the production of relative surplus value is immediately dependent upon improvements in productivity only in industries producing wage-goods – in itself a considerable part of the economy – the interdependence of one sort of production on another is such that improvements in productivity throughout the whole economy are in fact necessary. Second, there are the changes in the political and social fabric which the production of relative surplus value as the general mode of exploitation requires and, if anything, these are even more difficult to establish than the technical pre-conditions. We need only contrast conditions in Britain in the first part of the nineteenth century to see just how sweeping these changes are: the brutal oppression and endless hours of ill-paid work, the prohibition of trade unions and the disenfranchisement of the working class, with conditions today, to see that much more than an adjustment in real wages is necessary. In fact, the changes in the social situation of the working class that have proved necessary to establish the production of relative surplus value as the characteristic mode of exploitation are so profound that they have been widely mistaken for a revolutionary transformation of the mode of production itself which has ushered in some form of new post-capitalist industrial society.

Another application of absolute and relative surplus value as a criterion for distinguishing different forms of capitalism deserves some attention. Without in any way asserting that conditions today in what is called the underdeveloped world are identical to those of the advanced capitalist countries in the nineteenth century, there are, nevertheless, convincing grounds for characterising their mode of exploitation, in so far as it is established upon a fully capitalist basis, as the production of absolute surplus value. All the classic features of this mode of exploitation are present – the direct oppression of the working class in every sphere of social life. And the so-called problem of development consists precisely in the removal of these conditions without threatening the basis of capitalist production itself. In addition, since the production of relative surplus value leads to higher rates of surplus value, the rate of exploitation in the advanced countries is, generally speaking, higher than that in the underdeveloped world.

It is true that throughout most of the century between 1850 and 1950 large sectors of the economies of the underdeveloped world were not organised upon a capitalist basis properly speaking, and that their subordination to capital was organised indirectly through trade. But where capitalist production proper did develop, it employed labour-intensive forms of production which exploited labour at low levels of productivity. In these circumstances real wages were exceptionally low. In many parts of the underdeveloped world conditions have not changed all that much: in the mines of South Africa and the tea plantations of Sri Lanka modes of exploitation still exist which share more common features with Britain in the early nineteenth century than with the advanced world today. But new conditions are emerging which have already had dramatic effects upon the structure of the world economy and the working classes of the developed countries.

We refer here to what can only be described as the sudden growth after 1965 of new industries in parts of the underdeveloped world, most notably the countries of South and South East Asia such as Malaysia, Singapore, Hong Kong, Indonesia, the Phillipines, Taiwan and South

Korea, using advanced methods of production and turning out goods for western markets. The production of electronic goods is probably the best known, but many other items ranging from cars to shoes are involved. The innovatory feature of this industrialisation is that it is the first occasion on which methods of production associated with relative surplus value in the advanced countries have been transferred into the underdeveloped world where the political and social conditions of life are geared to the production of absolute surplus value. Asian workers do longer hours and earn much lower real wages than workers in the advanced countries, yet they are employed with modern techniques that make them equally productive. The attraction of this situation to business is obvious and capital has flooded into a region that combines the advantages of absolute and relative surplus value production in ways that are historically unprecedented. Although reliable data on employment in developing countries are not easily available – some probably have a more accurate account of the numbers of political prisoners than industrial workers – the pattern is unmistakeable, as the growth in employment in manufacturing industry in these countries has occurred while the relative number of workers so employed in the advanced capitalist countries has declined. In Britain between 1965 and 1974, an absolute decline was recorded in this category. Statistics never speak for themselves but the trend seems unmistakeable. Between 1965 and 1974 something in the order of 11 million new jobs in manufacturing industry were created globally and had these been distributed between the advanced capitalist countries and the underdeveloped world according to the ratio of 1965 the former would have got 8.8 million and the latter 2.2 million. In fact the advanced countries of Western Europe, N. America and Japan got only 4.5 million of these new jobs, and 6.5 million went to the underdeveloped world, the majority of the countries we mentioned above.

The recession that began in 1973–74 has obscured this tendency towards the global redistribution of world industry although it is significant to point out that the 'export' of jobs due to the redirection of investment is of such an order, that had the jobs been created in the advanced industrial countries unemployment today would have been substantially lower than it is, and something very close to the full employment levels of the post-war period would have been maintained.

5 Industrial Co-operation and Machine Production

In the last two chapters we have concentrated on production as the production of value and surplus value; now we must consider it as a material process which produces use-values. Ideally, capital would ignore this aspect of production since it is incidental to accumulation. In fact, it would ignore production altogether if that were possible and reduce its circuit to its bare essentials where money is circulated directly against money $(M - M')$. This is the ideal world of capital and periodically, in bouts of speculative fever, fantasy takes over as money chases profits far beyond the bounds of reasonable expectation. From the time of the South Sea Bubble to the latest junket with high-rise office blocks and Very Large Crude Carriers the irrationality of capital has regularly expressed itself in a genuine pathology as the frenzied pursuit of wealth in the abstract lays waste to the production of wealth in the concrete. These intermittent crises undoubtedly represent the quintessence of capital and illustrate more vividly than anything else, the human absurdity of organising social life round the principle of accumulation, but they tell us only part of the story. To grasp the historic significance of capital, we must see how it recognises the inevitability of material production and comes to terms with it. The first step is the formal control of production where capital includes it the movement of its own circuit. This is the historic transition from $M - C - M'$ where capital trades commodities produced outside its sphere of influence to $M - C^L_{MP} \ldots P \ldots C' - M'$ where production becomes capitalist production. As such, it becomes a value process which produces value and surplus value, though remaining first of all a material process that produces use-values. Thus capital can only achieve its ends indirectly through an activity that is not necessarily consistent with them. The history of capitalist production unfolds around an effort to minimise inconsistencies by organising material production in ways that are progressively more suitable to the requirements of accumulation. We call this the *adequation of material to value production*.

This adequation is a continuous process of reconstruction and adaptation, implemented by measures such as the development of new methods of production, the relocation of factories, the creation of new skills and then their extinction, and so on. In other words, it is a process made up of a mass of minute and apparently unrelated details. Nevertheless, a pattern is discernible in terms of the two criteria which stipulate capitalist success. First: the growth in productivity to reduce the value of labour-power to a minimum and increase the rate of surplus value to a maximum; and second: the organisation of production in ways that ensure that capital, through its hired managers, has the greatest possible degree of control over the living labour it employs. These criteria are not inevitably compatible with each other, but, to date, capital has achieved massive and undisputed success on both fronts through the adoption of two inter-related strategies which we must now examine in some detail – industrial co-operation and the application of machinery.

1. CO-OPERATION

The isolated worker, the craftsman or artisan who works alone as an individual productive unit, is exceptional in capitalist society whose characteristic form of work is *co-operation*, where many workers collaborate together in a collective work-force. The image of a group of workers collaborating and the idea of a team being something more than the individuals who comprise it, are easily grasped from everyday experience; but there are different forms of co-operation with different implications which cannot be appreciated quite so readily. To understand what these are, it is necessary to start with fundamentals and examine co-operation in terms of the *division of labour* – its most general and abstract form of existence.

But even the division of labour which appears so easy to define as an organisation of work whereby individuals do different things is not quite as straightforward as it seems. To understand the division of labour as the basis of co-operation in a way that allows us to identify different stages in the development of co-operation, we must make an elementary distinction between *simple* and *detailed division of labour*. There are many practical instances which blur this elementary distinction, nevertheless it is theoretically indispensable. A simple division of labour occurs when the output of an individual worker is an integral use-value, i.e. something that can be consumed as it stands. It does not matter whether consumption is personal or productive, only that the product is ready for use when the individual producer has finished with it. Thus the work of a tailor or a weaver is organised upon the basis of a simple division of labour so long as each works alone and the coat produced by the one and the cloth produced by the other can enter the process of circulation as a use-value in its own right. Where the division of labour is organised a detailed basis, this result no longer applies, as the product of the individual worker is no longer a distinguishable use-value. Contrast a tailor with the worker in a garment factory who spends her time cutting buttonholes and the point is at once clear. The detailed division of labour is not an invention of capitalist society, but it has been developed here more fully than ever before, providing the basis of industrial co-operation as it now exists.

Using this elementary distinction, we can now identify four stages in the development of co-operation.

1. *The Simple Division of Labour*: this is the division of labour as it exists in conditions of simple commodity production and all we need to do is remind ourselves of its basic features – the specialisation of individual producers and the isolated situation of their work. The most celebrated illustration of the division of labour is the pin factory with which Adam Smith began his *Enquiry into the Nature and Causes of the Wealth of Nations*. Pin-making, Adam Smith observed, required eighteen different processes such as drawing out the wire, straightening, cutting, pointing and grinding it and so on. Under the simple division of labour where individuals specialise in pin-making, but work alone, one man will carry out all eighteen processes himself.

2. *Elementary Co-operation*: this first step in the development of the division of labour sees the centralisation of pin-making, to retain this example, into a single factory, although production remains organised upon a strictly individual basis. Thus, although a group of pin makers are gathered under one roof, each one still makes complete pins himself, and the organisation of production proper is no different from the simple division of labour. It is unlikely that any such organisation of production has ever existed historically, but our concern here is with the logical structure of co-operation, rather than its historical development. Nevertheless, the first advantages of co-operation begin to appear even in these protean and somewhat abstract conditions. Already we can find definite signs of what economists call *economies of scale*. As the organisation and technology of the productive process remain un-

changed no direct improvements in productivity can be expected; but indirect savings in heating and lighting the work-place, in buying materials and selling the output, and so on, can be substantial. At the same time the advantages of centralisation for capital make their first appearance. Suppose that under conditions of the simple division of labour, individual pin-makers sell their product to a merchant capitalist who subsequently resells it. From the point of view of the capitalist the diffusion of production creates all manner of difficulties varying from quality control to the uncertainty of supplies. When production is gathered together in one place, particularly if that place belongs to the capitalist, and the pin-makers cease to be independent producers and become his employees, there are much greater possibilities for control. Thus even this most elementary form of co-operation (by simultaneously reducing costs and increasing the possibility of control), satisfies both capitalist criteria for production.

3. *Manufacturing Co-operation*: this form of co-operation corresponds to an actual historical phase of development. It is the one that Adam Smith observed at the dawn of capitalist production; he saw in it the division of labour, as such, emphasising the enormous increases in productivity it made possible. Now the division of labour becomes more detailed, and in place of being a pin-maker, the worker concentrates on one or two operations only. Thus one man draws out the wire, another cuts it, a third sharpens it and so on; as pin-making is turned from an individual into a genuinely collective project. The increase in production, Smith noted, was dramatic: when 10 men worked individually, total output never exceeded 200 pins a day; when they specialised in one or two operations and worked collectively, production rose to 48,000. The scale of this increase may be exceptional, but there can be no doubting the growth in productivity that such reorganisation can achieve. Applied across the board its advantages for capital are evident: a general growth in productivity reduces the value of all commodities including wage-goods, hence it reduces the value of labour-power and increases the rate of surplus value. But this is only part of the story.

The development of manufacturing co-operation introduces a seminal change in the division of labour and the new form of labour-process it engenders is an essential prerequisite for capitalist production. As a social form of production, capitalism has *formal* conditions – generalised commodity production with its attendant legal and political structures, and the buying and selling of labour-power which requires a social distribution of property that condemns the great mass of the people to absolute poverty. But these formal conditions are insufficient by themselves, and capitalist production proper only begins when they are complemented by an adequate form of material production. That is to say, the formal conditions of capitalism, the social relations of production that are encapsulated in the transaction between the capitalist and the worker, i.e. the wage, can only exist historically where production, as a material process that creates use-values, is organised in a fashion consistent with them. This point is not as abstruse as it may appear and one aspect of this consistency can be readily illustrated. The existence of labour as wage-labour involves the absolute poverty of the great mass of the people; or, to say the same thing, it involves a system of social distribution that puts the great mass of wealth into the hands of a small minority of the population. But how can any minority exercise power over a majority unless its individual members are each able to control large numbers? If an individual capitalist could effectively control only one worker, or at best a few, directly through employment, capitalism as a fully developed social form of production simply could not exist. To put the point positively, capitalist production proper requires the individual capitalist to control a large number of workers and this, in turn, requires methods of production that aggregate substantial numbers of workers together into large cohesive labour-forces. Methods of production which rest upon an individual labour-process simply will not do. If the division of labour is not developed beyond its elementary form, producers remain scattered in isolated units, probably their homes, and a single capitalist is unable to supervise more than a few, leaving large numbers with an intolerable degree of freedom. Even simple cooperation is insufficient, for although this gathers workers into factories and removes the spatial difficulties of supervision, the individual nature of the work still limits detailed control. Manufacturing co-operation clears all these obstacles out of the way and provides the starting point of capitalist production proper. By aggregating relatively large numbers of workers into single labour forces it allows individual capitalists to employ many workers in conditions conducive to a detailed and rigorous control of work.

To develop this line of analysis further and express it in appropriate general terms, we must understand exactly what changes manufacturing co-operation brings about in the division of labour. Adam Smith's pin factory is a most useful vehicle for this, though interestingly enough neither Adam Smith nor the economists who have followed him down to the present day, have drawn the obvious conclusions. In fact, Smith himself is more open to the issue than contemporary economists whose

Industrial Co-operation and Machine Production

narrow preoccupation with the quantitative dimension of economic life causes them to treat the division of labour exclusively in terms of its effects upon productivity. This neglect of qualitative changes in the labour-process is reinforced by a general reluctance to acknowledge capitalist society as a political structure that confers power upon a small minority. The uncritical view that it consists of a mass of independent individuals could not withstand an examination of manufacturing co-operation which undermines the real basis of this individuality.

To see the qualitative results of changes in the division of labour, it is necessary to put the quantitative ones aside and so, for the moment, let us assume the level of productivity remains constant. Suppose 10 men can produce 1,000 pins in two different circumstances; one where the division of labour has not progressed beyond its simple form and another where co-operation is organised upon a manufacturing basis. In other words, consider two situations where the level of output and productivity is the same but the organisation of the labour process is different. In one case each of the 10 men perform all 18 processes that pin-making requires; in the other, they perform only one or two operations. Clearly production in the first case is *individual*, even if the producers are gathered together under the same roof; in the second case it is no less clearly *collective*. The different ways in which total output is computed in the two cases illustrates this point conveniently. Under conditions of simple co-operation where the division of labour is still organised on a rudimentary basis, total output is calculated by adding the outputs of the individual workers – the output of the first worker plus the output of the second and so on. But with manufacturing co-operation this precedure is no longer possible, since individual workers no longer produce pins. When productivity is to be compared, the appropriate procedure is to contrast average output per head in the two situations. That is to say, we make a calculation in terms of the output of the *average worker*. But we must not confuse this average worker with the *individual worker*; average workers in the arithmetical sense always exist, but not individual workers. This may appear another obscure distinction but again it is a crucially important one. By an individual worker we mean one whose product has sufficient integrity as a use-value to go on to the market as it stands and confront other commodities as a value. A pin, for example, is already a fully formed use-value, and if it is produced by a single worker we can say he is an individual worker. But a piece of sharpened wire, a pin-head or any other component product, does not have the same integrity, and the worker who produces them does not have individuality in this sense. When the lines along which labour is divided correspond to actual use-values, we have a simple division of labour and individual workers; but where the division of labour extends beyond this point to the detailed division of labour which is characteristic of manufacturing co-operation, the individual worker no longer exists as such. With the simple division of labour the subject of production is the individual worker; with the detailed division of labour it is the *collective worker*, the organised group of workers into which the individual is subsumed as a mere constituent element.

It is true that the constituent elements of the collective worker are human individuals who each have their own unique features, their own hopes and fears, tastes and ambitions; but as members of the collective workforce, their individuality is irrelevant. As the language of the factory has it, they are 'hands' or 'operatives' or simply 'workers', and individuality in work is reduced to a numerical abstraction – the total workforce divided by the number in it. This emasculated individual is simply a *worker-in-general*; a fragment of humanity who, as a worker, is no different from other fragments who sell their labour-power in return for a wage and we shall refer to him as the *general* or *average worker*.

The question now arises of the relationship between the activity of the general worker and abstract labour that produces value. At first sight the two appear identical and it is tempting to follow those writers who argue that the labour performed by the general worker – *general labour* – is only abstract labour by another name. But this appealing conclusion that concrete labour has become so routine and repetitive that it has lost all its distinguishing features and become merely a mechanical activity, labour as such and hence abstract labour, is based upon a profound misunderstanding of economic categories. Concrete labour, no matter how dull, boring and unskilled, is always concrete labour engaged in material production. On the other hand, highly skilled labour, even if it is performed individually, becomes abstract labour when its product is sold as a commodity. Thus it is not the nature of concrete labour that makes it abstract labour: this depends upon the social form assumed by the product outside the sphere of production. On the other hand, the ease or difficulty of organising concrete labour according to the requirements of this form, vary among different types of concrete labour and the point we are making is that the type of generalised labour engendered by manufacturing co-operation is easier to organise for this purpose than any other.

If the division of labour had never developed beyond its simple form, capitalist production (which we can now define as the imposition of the discipline of value, i.e. abstract labour, directly on concrete labour in the sphere of production) could never have developed, since producers would have maintained their individuality at work and therefore potential independence of capital in society at large. By destroying the individual worker, manufacturing co-operation destroys the potentially independent producer and this is an indispensible condition of capitalist production. In general theoretical terms, we can draw the following conclusions: *first*, manufacturing co-operation and the detailed division of labour it engenders, represents the first step towards organising the process of material production in a form that is adequate to the production of value; and second, the average or general workers who make up the collective workforce lose their individuality which has no place in a society where work is organised on the basis of abstract labour.

4. *Industrial Co-operation*: here all the advantages to capital of manufacturing co-operation are consolidated and increased many times by revolutionary changes in the productive process that introduce new techniques adequate to the collective organisation of labour. Industrial co-operation differs from manufacturing co-operation on exactly those grounds that manufacturing and simple co-operation share.

In any process of development, whether logical or historical, the shift from one phase to the next never involves a complete and abrupt transformation. The new phase, however different in some respects from the one it replaces, always embodies elements of it, thus giving continuity in change. If we think of a process of change that has three definite phases, it is often the case that what changes between the second and third phase is that which is unchanged between the first and second. The development of co-operation fits neatly into this pattern as industrial co-operation on the one hand, retains the novel features of manufacturing co-operation, but on the other, realises new possibilities that were only previously latent. The retained features are the detailed division of labour and the replacement of the individual by the collective worker as the subject of production; to grasp the new features we must go back and find what it is that manufacturing co-operation has in common with simple co-operation. Adam Smith's pin factory again provides us with all the information we need.

The changes involved in the shift from simple to manufacturing co-operation are clear enough. The most important is the reorganisation of the division of labour on a detailed basis, whereby a worker performs only one, or at the most two or three, of the eighteen processes that pin-making requires. The point we must stress is that this reorganisation does not change the process of production in any fundamental way. The technology of production remains what it was. Pin-making still requires the same eighteen processes: the content of work is exactly what it was under simple co-operation; only its distribution among the workers has changed. In so far as this is the case, an incongruency arises between technology and the organisation of the workforce, the former being based on individual production, while the latter is ordered among the collective worker. Industrial co-operation resolves this inconsistency.

Two phases can be identified in the development of capitalist production. In the first, capital seizes control of production as it is already organised on a non-capitalist basis and subjects it to its formal control; by turning independent producers into wage-labourers, gathering them into factories – simple co-operation; and then reorganising the labour-process – manufacturing co-operation. But throughout this transition the technology of production remains unchanged, and however revolutionary the new factories may be, their potential is limited so long as they rely upon a technology rooted in the past when the active agent of production was the individual producer. First, the scale of production is restricted as the factory owner can only add together parallel processes and not develop new ones that start from the collective nature of the work. Second, this restriction on scale limits the development of productivity, and hence limits the growth of the rate of surplus value which is the whole aim of the exercise. The capitalist urge to accumulate confronts material production as a barrier and hence continually reorganises it to improve efficiency. In this reorganisation it is possible to distinguish theoretically between a recomposition on the basis of a given technology and a reorganisation of the technological base. The developments which are widely referred to as the Industrial Revolution involved a reorganisation of the latter sort, as the previously established capitalist relations of production broke down the barriers to the growth of surplus value by establishing material production upon an industrial basis. Third, so long as technology bears the imprint of individual production, detailed capitalist control over production remains limited. This is because of the central and active role played by living labour. Manufacturing co-operation which consolidates the detailed division of labour simplifies supervision greatly, since it is much easier to keep an eye on a worker and check his performance if the tasks he is set are narrowly defined. But the productive process even under these conditions starts from the capacities of living workers, and to this extent the capitalist cannot define the content of work in all its details, and cannot, therefore, control it in all its aspects. Only when production becomes a totally capitalist project, when capital determines the technology to be used independently of living labour whose autonomous skills are made irrelevant; only when living labour is displaced as the active agent from the centre of production whose material content in all its details, as well as its social form, is determined by capital; only then does the capitalist mode of production begin to develop properly on its own foundations. It is clear that this only happens with the development and widespread application of machinery, and a moment's reflection shows that machine production overcomes the other limitations of manufacturing co-operation by increasing both productivity and the scale of production.

2. MACHINERY

A machine is easily recognised and distinguished from less elaborate instruments of production; thus bulldozers and combine harvesters are clearly machines, as opposed to spades and scythes which are simply tools. But common sense is as unreliable here as elsewhere. On this question it tends to adopt a narrow technical point of view which is quite inadequate for understanding *machinery in capitalist society*. The technical features of machinery and their effect upon living labour reproduce in physical terms the social relations of capitalism so closely that there are strong grounds for viewing machinery exclusively in this light. Non-capitalist societies have certainly produced contraptions that bear many of the hallmarks of machines, as for example the medieval water-mill; but this hardly throws the specifically capitalist nature of machinery into doubt, since it is only in capitalist society that machinery has been systematically developed and applied to production on a large scale. What is beyond dispute is that the three most important technical features of machines make them peculiarly suitable to serve as instruments of capitalist production. They are:

1. In contrast to a simple tool the machine has its own independent source of power. Where it is the muscle of the living producer that forces the spade and swings the scythe, bulldozers and combine-harvesters have their own motors. The first machines to be used on a wide scale were in the textile industry in Britain at the end of the eighteenth century, but authorities agree that mechanised production proper only began in the nineteenth century when the new spinning and weaving machines were attached to steam engines. Subsequently steam was replaced by electricity and the internal combustion engine, but the principle remains the same: with its own independent source of power the pace and rhythm at which a machine works is not determined by the energy or inclinations of

the workers. On the contrary, the machine imposes the pace and rhythm of work upon the worker, and by definition, these are non-human. We need not dwell on this aspect of the question long to see its great advantages for capital. The capitalist employs a worker and pays him the value of his labour-power. He then equips him with a tool, say a spade, and sets him to work. From this moment on the amount of work actually done is very much in the worker's hands. His strength determines the maximum he can achieve but all manner of other factors come into play to reduce the actual amount he does below this level. The capitalist can attempt to counter these by close supervision, the payment of piece-rates and the like, but since the worker's own energy is the source of power, the pace of production is ultimately determined by him. The introduction of mechanised means of production tilts the balance in favour of the capitalist. With the most developed form of mechanised production, the conveyor belt, the worker loses all direct control of how much he does, and capital is able to supervise him directly through the instrument of production itself. It is true that not all spheres of production are mechanised in this way, and that even where they are, workers do not passively accept the pace of work that machines impose upon them. Disputes about the speed of machines are common, and where no agreement can be struck between managers and workers, the latter frequently retaliate through neglect and, at times, outright sabotage to stop the line. Notwithstanding this, the fact remains that the technical capacity of machines to power themselves denies the worker autonomy in controlling the pace of his work, and, to this extent, puts greater control into the hands of capital. In return for the value he pays for labour-power, the capitalist who employs his workers on machines can be sure of getting more work out of them than the capitalist who supplies his workers with tools; hence more value and surplus value.

2. Because it has its own source of power the head of the machine, the part that comes into direct contact with the material to be worked, need make no concession to the natural capabilities of the human operative. With a simple tool things are completely different. The blade of a scythe, for instance, is shaped so that it can be wielded by a man who provides its power; but the blades of a harvester that are driven by a motor move in a rotary fashion that human energy cannot easily drive. Here, as elsewhere, there are no clear-cut dividing lines, and the simple lawnmower neatly bisects the gap between what is clearly a tool on the one side, and what is a machine on the other. But there is little point exploring the grey areas that inevitably fall between definitions when the principle involved is clear. The inevitable corollary of machinery having a power source that is

Industrial Co-operation and Machine Production 65

independent of the human operative is that other parts of the machine develop in the same non-human fashion. As the head evolves in this way, a decisive change is introduced into the labour process and the living worker is removed from the centre of the productive process – direct contact with the material. Three implications of this change are especially important for us here.

First, the special construction of the head of the machine coupled with its independent power source, which not only drives it but directs it with the appropriate pressure, makes traditional artisan skill redundant. Where shaping a piece of metal by hand with the use of tools requires considerable dexterity by the workman, as well as a knowledge of metal that can only be acquired from long experience, the operator of a numerically controlled machine requires no special manual skills, no knowledge of the materials being worked and very little training. Skill, defined in the traditional sense as the ability to work materials, becomes the property of the machine; while the worker becomes a mere attendant who feeds it materials, services its needs and collects its output. But if skill becomes the property of the machine, it becomes also the property of the capitalist who owns the machine; in other words, with the use of machinery capital appropriates the human content of work and finds it that much easier to subordinate it to its own ends – the production of surplus value.

Second, in so far as the labour that works directly with machinery is 'deskilled' and training time reduced to an absolute minimum, workers become easily interchangeable. This development greatly facilitates the growth of an open labour market which favours the capitalist more than workers to the extent that the latter lack a defined technical basis on which to organise and regulate 'supply'.

Third, although the 'deskilling' of labour directly employed on machinery has played such a decisive role in capitalist development its importance should not be exaggerated. The old skill of the artisan no longer plays any serious part in production, and the widespread use of machinery has certainly introduced a new category of producer into economic history in the form of the mass unskilled worker. But it has not destroyed skill altogether, but rather changed its nature. Whereas skill in the pre-capitalist epoch involved an ability to handle materials and was usually acquired by producers as part of their general experience of life, skill in the capitalist epoch generally requires a knowledge of machinery, which can only be acquired under the auspices of capital. Furthermore, skill in many cases is *job-specific*; and the abilities a worker acquires not only come through his employment by capital in relation to objects that belong to capital, but are frequently acquired through employment by an individual capitalist and have limited relevance elsewhere. In other words, capital regulates the market for skilled labour in exactly the opposite way from that of unskilled labour: with the latter it develops a broad market, with the former a very narrow one.

3. The use of machinery increases the scale of production but also standardises the product. We have already discussed the necessity of large-scale production whereby one capital can employ many workers for the maintenance of capitalist power in society as a whole. The increases in productivity that large-scale production makes possible, and the positive effects they have on the rate of surplus value, are so obvious that we need to do no more than mention them. We will therefore direct our attention to the standardisation of production that mechanisation makes possible and without which large-scale production would be impossible.

The advantages of standardisation within the productive process in facilitating quality control and reducing waste through the use of interchangeable parts, are also obvious; but what are much less apparent are the benefits that standardisation brings to capital outside the sphere of production. We need only recall that the social power of capital in the advanced countries, particularly in the period since the Second World War, has rested upon the twin pillars of working class affluence and the replacement of genuine individuality by an abstract facsimile of itself, to realise the importance of standardisation, especially in the production of wage-goods. In the twentieth century the machine has left the factory and become an object of consumption; and while it would be a figurative exaggeration to claim that it has turned society into a factory, the advantages it has brought to capital outside the factory certainly parallel those it has brought within. Nowhere are these more noticeable than in the redefinition of the individual citizen as the motorist, the viewer, the consumer. While the possession of the consumer-machine becomes a mark of prestige, and the choice of which machine to possess the proof of individual freedom, the standardisation of the product into batches of millions that are identical, and other batches that differ only in inconsequential detail, contains both this affluence and individuality within the dull uniformity of capitalist power. No better description of late capitalism exists than the bourgeoise nightmare of communism as a society of monotonous uniformity; only in capitalist society uniformity masquerades as diversity and servitude as freedom.

It is the cumulation of these advantages that machinery bestows upon capital – the improvements in productivity that make possible increases in the rate of surplus value; the control of labour by determining the pace and rhythm of work, by deskilling here and redefining skill there; and the standardisation of social life outside the factory through the medium of mass consumption and its corrollary, mass culture, that gives the argument that machinery is a specifically capitalist phenomenon such persuasive power. When the social consequences of machinery are fully acknowledged, it becomes hard to see its development in neutral technical terms. It is true that machinery is a technical phenomenon and the development of new machines is a technical exercise often undertaken with no social or class motive in mind. But the evolution and development of machinery as such, can hardly be a merely technical development that just fortuitously turned out well for capital. Too much evidence points in the other direction, and the grounds for rejecting the view that machinery is the adequate form of capital – to be precise, constant capital in the instruments of production – and for this reason inadequate, or inappropriate, for a mode of production not based upon capital, seem slight and insubstantial.

The revolutionary conclusion of this analysis, the *abolition of machinery*, is not as naive or utopian as it first appears. As a peculiarly capitalist instrument of production, the technical characteristics of machinery that count are those which allow large numbers of unskilled or semi-skilled workers to be centralised and controlled in one place. But it is precisely these characteristics that the most recent developments in technology appear to be undermining. The type of factory already foreshadowed by the latest advances in microelectronics is one that dispenses with the great mass of workers, retaining only a few highly trained supervisory staff. Already the alarms are being sounded about the dangers of this method of production, particularly the threat of large-scale unemployment whose economic significance we will consider in Chapter 8. But the question that springs most readily to mind concerns the nature of a society that can even anticipate with foreboding new technologies that promise to free large sections of the population from the treadmill of dull and monotonous work. The answer offers itself immediately: a society organised upon just such a basis; one whose social relations are most adequately expressed in material terms by mass, dull, routine labour that robs the worker of his individuality. Behind the specific anxieties about the consequences of automation is one general, if unconscious, fear: that the new techniques of production are not machines in the historical sense; hence not adequate for capitalist production but capable of providing a suitable basis for a society based upon free labour.

6 Wages

We must now examine the important economic categories of capitalist society in greater detail. In the next chapter we look at profits; here our subject is wages. The main question we must consider is one already touched upon in Section 2 of Chapter 4, how it is possible for real wages to rise at the same time as the rate of exploitation. But before this we must understand exactly what wages are and look at what is called the *wage-form*.

1. THE WAGE-FORM

We have seen on several occasions how common sense makes an unreliable guide to economic and social life, since things are rarely what they seem to be. In the case of wages, the discrepancy between reality and appearance is clear-cut and it is easy to understand why it is actually necessary; why wages must appear as something altogether different from what they are. Elsewhere it is not so clear-cut, but the wage is only one in a series of interrelated economic categories that includes profits, prices and money, to name the most important, and anything that affects one member of the series must affect them all. For this reason the discrepancy between appearance and reality which we will analyse exclusively in terms of the wage-form must be recognised as a systematic feature of capitalist society. *Fetishism*, to call it by its proper name, finds its ultimate origins in the commodity nature of capitalist production.

Daily experience tells us that wages are the *value or price of labour*. Thus if a worker is paid on a time basis he gets so much per hour; if he is paid piece-rates his wage is calculated in terms of how much he produces. Both forms of payment contradict the theoretical definition of wages as the value of labour-power, according to which workers are not paid for the work they do, but the value necessary to do this work – i.e. they are paid according to the value of the means of consumption necessary for them to work. Moreover, the view that wages are the value of labour implies that workers are paid not only according to the amount of work they do, but that they are paid for everything they do, and that therefore they are not exploited at work. It follows from this that no such thing as surplus value can exist and the origins of profit must be sought elsewhere – in the buying and selling of commodities or the contribution made to production by machinery. On the other hand we have seen that profits cannot be anything but surplus value produced by living labour. But if surplus value is the difference between the value produced by labour and the value paid as wages, the workers cannot be paid the full value of what they produce. This is the problem: profits are surplus value and surplus value requires workers to be paid only a portion of what they produce. Wages are indisputably paid according to the amount of work done. How can what is necessarily true be reconciled with what is evidently true?

In Chapter 3 we set up an example where 1,500 workers are employed for 40 hours a week, 50 weeks a year giving a total of 3 million hours. Assuming that 1 hour of labour produces a value of £1, living labour in these circumstances produces a new value of £3 million. At the same time we assumed that the items of consumption needed to support the workers take 1.5 million hours to produce: this made the value of labour-power. the amount paid to the workers as wages, £1.5 million. But to earn this amount the workers had to work 3 million hours: that is to say, they had to produce a new value of £3 million to earn wages of £1.5 million. Now this does not present itself as a practical problem to either the capitalist or the worker for both parties can make the calculations that concern them on the basis of the *wage* rate (50p per hour), and treat this rate as though it were an independent variable. The capitalist works out how many man hours he requires for a year, multiplies this by the going wage-rate and calculates the amount of variable capital he needs; the workers multiply the wage-rate by the hours put in to calculate their earnings. The determination of the wage-rate is naturally important to both parties, but both tend to see it simply in bargaining terms and pay little attention to underlying economic conditions. At one time, governments were prepared to adopt the same attitude and let free collective bargaining take care of itself; but in recent years this has proved impossible and intervention has occurred through income policies of one sort or another. The official account of these policies is the reconciliation of individual pay deals with national economic requirements: its unconscious purpose is to reconcile wage-rates (the value of labour) with the value of labour-power. The problem of determining wages through negotiations over wage-rates is that the value of labour can exceed the value of labour-power and bring down the rate of surplus value. The undeclared aim of incomes policies is to make sure that this does not happen.

Thus, it turns out that the value of labour is more than a false and misleading appearance of wages. Workers are indeed paid according to the amount of work they do, and it is in terms of the value of labour that wage negotiations take place. In acknowledging this fact at the same time as it recognises that wages are the value of labour-power, the *wage-form* is a duality that combines the nature of the wage with its form of existence. In our example, where the wage-rate multiplied by the number of hours worked equals the value of labour-power, this duality is hidden and has no practical significance; but this inequality is far from inevitable in what economists call the short period. It is quite possible for wage negotiations to result in wage-rates (i.e. value of labour) that do not equal the value of labour-power. Suppose a successful strike occurs in our car factory and the workers win a rise of 10p per hour, while all the conditions of production stay the same. Under these new circumstances the wage bill goes up to £1.8 million (3 million hours @ 60p per hour) although the value of labour-power is still £1.5 million. The qualitative difference between the two aspects of the wage becomes quantitative and makes itself felt to the capitalist in the one way that really matters – a fall in profits. If this happens in only one firm the repercussions are not serious, except of course for the firm in question; but if it happens throughout the economy some general adjustment is inevitable. In the traditional conditions of capitalism prevailing in the nineteenth century, governments tended to stand aloof from the labour market, which was left to deal with this type of imbalance in its own way. Obliged to pay higher wage-rates, the fall in profitability hits less efficient firms most severely, forcing them to cut down operations and lay off workers. Depending upon the extent to which the value of labour exceeded the value of labour-power and conditions prevailing in the labour market, this generalised itself into a depression that lasted until unemployment finally forced wage-rates back into line with the value of labour-power and profits were returned to what the economists euphemistically call their normal level. If unemployment is politically unacceptable, at least on a scale sufficient to reconcile the two aspects of the wage, then direct government intervention in the labour market through incomes policy, becomes inevitable. For these reasons the distinction between the value of labour-power and the value of labour is more than a fine theoretical distinction with little practical significance; on the contrary, its existence is one of the main conditions of capitalist instability.

But if this is the case, why, we may ask, does the wage have this double aspect? Why does the value of labour-power exist as the value of labour? Why does it not exist as itself, for surely it would be in the interests of capital to negotiate with workers in terms of the money they need to buy their means of necessary consumption? If wages were negotiated on these terms, the system would be saved a great deal of confusion and instability, to the benefit of all classes. On the other hand, without confusion and instability capitalism would not be what it is, and the ambiguity of the wage-form which creates the possibility of so many problems is intrinsic in its nature. At least it is intrinsic to the buying and selling of labour-power which, for all intents and purposes, is to say the same thing.

Like any other commodity, labour-power which the worker sells to the capitalist is only potential use-value, but from this point all similarities between labour-power and other commodities end. First, the realised use-value of labour-power, labour, unlike the realised use-value of any other commodity, creates value. But it is a second peculiarity of the use-value, labour-power, that matters here. Suppose I am a tailor: the coat I produce is a potential use-value and my customer buys it for this reason, so that in consuming the coat he can realise this potential as warmth, style or whatever. But my business with him ends when the transaction is complete; and so it is with all commodities except labour-power. When a worker sells his labour-power to a capitalist the formal conclusion of the transaction marks only the beginning of their relationship, since the realisation of the use-value of labour-power, unlike that of any other commodity, requires the personal presence of its seller – the worker. In fact it requires not just his presence, but his active participation, and the capitalist has no guarantee that this will be given voluntarily or to the extent desired. The problem of transforming labour-power into labour has existed as long as capitalism itself, and the development of the detailed division of labour, and the application of machinery which we discussed in the last chapter, are among the more important means capital has evolved to deal with it. The system of payment, where the wage becomes the value of labour is another. Wages, unlike the prices of other commodities, are paid not at the time of purchase but later, when labour-power has been satisfactorily consumed. In every other case payment takes place when the commodity is still a potential use-value: thus bread is paid for before it is eaten; clothes, before they are worn and so on. Sometimes, with hire purchase for example, payment is delayed until the process of consumption has begun, but it is always completed before this process is finished, and in no way is it conditional upon the commodity giving satisfaction. At other times there are guarantees and the customer can get his money back, or have repairs done free if the commodity does not give full satisfaction. But guarantees never cover the full life of the commodity and their similarities with the conditions surrounding the buying and selling of labour-power are not as close as they appear. Labour-power is the only commodity whose seller is paid after full consumption has occurred, on condition of its consumption being satisfactory, and then *pro rata* with consumption. The reason for this is obvious: it is only by paying the worker after the use-value of labour-power is realised that the capitalist can be sure of getting anything for his money. The practice is so firmly established that buying and selling labour-power in the same way as other commodities, i.e. payment in advance, would appear absurd.

Thus it is the peculiarity of labour-power as a commodity whose use-value can only be realised in the presence and with the active participation of its seller, which gives rise to the special form of wage payment. From this it follows that the wage as the value of labour stems directly from the buying and selling of labour-power; and since this is the *specifica differentia* of capitalism, the duality of the wage-form arises from the mode of production itself. Another way of putting this is to say that the duality of the wage-form is the only way of accommodating the problems that arise when a human attribute is bought and sold as though it were a thing. But as capitalist production rests upon precisely this peculiarity, of dealing with human capacities as though they were things, the simplification of the wage-form to its essence (the value of labour-power) is impossible, and it must continue to exist as the value of labour with all the difficulties this implies.

In addition to its practical functions, the duality of the wage-form plays the indispensable ideological role of obscuring exploitation. For as we have seen, when wages are paid as the value of labour it appears that they are paid for everything they do and not just for the things they need in order to work.

2. THE 'IMMISERATION' OF LABOUR

In our analysis of relative surplus value in Chapter 4 we saw how a rise in productivity which reduces the value of wage-goods makes possible increases in both real wages and the rate of surplus value, and it is convenient to reproduce the numerical example we used to illustrate this point.

	Initial situation	Productivity doubled in wage-goods sector
	(1)	(2)
real wage (index)	100	150
value of wage (hours)	4	3
surplus value (hours)	4	5
rate of surplus value (per cent)	100	166

Given an initial situation where the rate of surplus value is 100 per cent, a doubling of productivity in the wage-goods sector allows real wages to rise by 50 per cent and the rate of surplus by 66 per cent. A clear advantage accrues to capital but the workers also make some gains. The value of labour-power falls, but in the circumstances this is not particularly significant, as the two aspects of the wage which are immediately important for the workers, the real wage and the value of labour, both rise. Consider the following:

$$\text{value of labour} = \frac{\text{real wage}}{\text{total number of hours worked}}$$

Total hours worked equals necessary labour time plus surplus labour time, that is the value of the wage plus surplus value expressed in hours. In both cases this equals 8 hours, but the real wage rises from 100 in the first case to 150 and the value of labour increases proportionately. In other words, for performing the same amount of labour the workers are paid a wage that allows them to buy 50 per cent more commodities. Set against this, a 25 per cent fall in the value of labour-power is not noticeable – at least not to the workers. The capitalists notice it as an increase in the rate of surplus value.

This combination of effects whereby the workers gain through a rise in the value of labour and the capitalists through a fall in the value of labour-power, indicates a further way in which the double nature of the wage serves to stabilise class relations. But, it must be stressed, it is only an increase in productivity that can take advantage of it, since it is only increases in productivity that can increase the value of labour at the same time as the value of labour-power falls. When labour is *intensified* different relations exist and the same possibilities of class harmony do not prevail.

So far we have taken *duration* as the sole measure of labour, talking of 1 hour's labour, 2 hours', 8 hours' and so on. Now we must recognise that in the space of an hour, to take this as the unit, a worker can do more or less work. If discipline in a factory is slack, workers tend to do less than when it is strict: thus a working day of 8 hours in a carefully organised and tightly supervised factory invariably results in more work than in another, where organisation is poor and supervision leaves the workers greater freedom. Equally, in factories where the methods of production depend upon positive initiatives by the workers, the pace of work and the amount of work done tends to be less than where the instruments of production play the active part and set the pace of work. This is one of the attractions of machinery to capital and mechanisation is one of the most important methods it uses to intensify labour. As labour is intensified, an increase takes place in the amount of work done during the day, even though the number of hours worked remains the same. Thus a doubling of intensity on the basis of a given period of labour, say 8 hours, counts as a doubling of labour: it is as though only 4 hours were worked in the one case and 8 hours in the second (or 8 hours and 16 hours depending upon what we take as the base). Either way the result is the same: intensification increases the amount of labour expended and therefore the value produced.

It is easy to confuse the intensification of labour with increases in productivity partly because they invariably occur together in practice and partly because their immediate effects upon output are similar. When productivity is doubled, output goes up by 100 per cent, and exactly the same happens when the intensity of labour is increased at the same rate. But this similarity masks an important difference. When productivity increases, a constant amount of labour produces a greater output, but as this greater output contains no more labour than the smaller output that preceded it, it contains no more value. In other words a rise in productivity increases the volume of use-values produced, but the value produced remains constant: hence there is a fall in the value of individual commodities. This we have seen several times already. With an increase in the intensity of labour both output and labour expended increase by the same proportion; hence the ratio of use-values to value produced remains constant and the value of individual commodities is unchanged.

Suppose a factory where a worker produces 4 shirts in 8 hours. If for the sake of convenience we leave out the value contributed by the means of production, each shirt has a value of 2 hours. Now assume that productivity doubles while the intensity of labour is unchanged. In 8 hours the worker now produces 8 shirts so that the value of each shirt falls by half to one hour. Next, starting from the same conditions assume the intensity of labour is doubled but productivity remains constant.

Twice as many shirts are produced, but in the 8 hours of the working day twice as much work is done. In producing the 8 shirts it is as though the worker has worked for 16 hours, and whichever way we calculate it the fact remains that each shirt contains the same amount of labour as it did previously, and therefore has the same value. Intensification and improvements in productivity also affect wages and surplus value differently.

The following schema is similar to the one used above to illustrate the affects of changes in productivity.

	Initial situation (1)	Intensity of labour doubled (2)
real wage (index)	100	100
value of wage (hours)	4	4
surplus value (hours)	4	12
rate of surplus value (per cent)	100	300

We assume that the intensity of labour is doubled and that the level of real wages remains constant. As intensification does nothing to change the value of commodities it follows that the value of labour-power does not change. But whereas 4 hours of unintensified labour represents half the working day in situation (1), giving a rate of surplus value of 100 per cent; in situation (2) where twice as much work is done (the equivalent of 16 hours), 4 of which are still sufficient to produce the equivalent of necessary consumption, leaving 12 hours over as surplus and giving a rate of surplus value of 300 per cent.

Now assume that the workers are able to improve their position by forcing up real wages by 50 per cent: the same thing we assumed to have happened when productivity was doubled.

	Initial situation (1)	Intensity of labour doubled (2)
real wage (index)	100	150
value of wage (hours)	4	6
surplus value (hours)	4	10
rate of surplus value (per cent)	100	166

(We have again taken the unintensified hour of situation (1) as the unit of measurement so that the working day when intensity is doubled contains 16 hours.)

At first sight, these results appear identical to those we had earlier when productivity rose: the real wage has risen from 100 to 150 and the rate of surplus value from 100 to 166 per cent. One anomaly is that the value of the wage has also risen by 50 per cent showing that the apparently impossible can happen – i.e. the value of labour-power and the rate of surplus value can both rise at the same time. But it is another aspect of the situation that must claim our attention for the moment. What has happened to the value of labour?

We have seen that the value of labour is the ratio of real wages to hours worked. In situation (1) this is 100:8 hours. The real wage now goes up to 150 but what of hours worked? The working day still lasts for 8 hours but in this time the workers do twice as much work and, measured in old hours, this new day counts as though it were 16 hours long. The new value of labour is therefore 150:16 hours which is a drop of 25 per cent on what it was. The workers do twice as much work for a wage that is only 50 per cent greater. Although their basket of consumer goods is bigger at the end of the day, for every item in that basket the worker has had to do 25 per cent more work. This is one explanation why rising real wages have not brought about the peaceful industrial relations that might have been expected, and why so many strikes and stoppages in the post-war period have been called over conditions of work. For with the intensification of labour it is through modifications in these conditions – more detailed supervision, reduced manning, faster machine speeds and so on – that increased rates of exploitation are achieved. And to the extent this takes place, wages struggles cannot be contained within formal bargaining arrangements; or to put it another way, when the intensification of labour occupies a central place in the strategy of exploitation, the immediate struggle between capital and the working class over the distribution of income continually threatens the framework of formal wage negotiations and the machinery of collective bargaining, since the crucial confrontations take place beyond their scope at shop-floor level. The relative failures of government sponsored incomes policy in the fifties and sixties; the growing inability throughout this period of trade unions to guarantee their members adherence to national agreements; the growth of wildcat strikes and unofficial stoppages relative to official strikes; the shift of power away from the established union bureaucracies to shop stewards and beyond them to the factory floor; all indicate the extent to which wages struggles are fought over conditions of work.

The reduction in the value of labour which is necessary to any successful strategy of intensification confirms the position that any gains

Wages 77

made by capital in increasing the rate of surplus value must involve some loss to the working class; and that it is impossible for both capital and the working class to make clear and unambiguous gains at the same time. This is the essence of the thesis of the growing *immiseration* of the working class. The successful realisation by capital of its innate drive to accumulation on an ever expanding scale can only be achieved at the expense of the working class which alone produces value, surplus value and hence capital itself. In the last analysis, an increase in the rate of surplus value must always cause the wage to fall in one or other of its aspects: with increasing productivity it is the wage as the value of labour-power that falls; with intensification, the wage as the value of labour.

The schemata used here are artificial constructs designed to illustrate the effects of changes in productivity and intensification in the most general and abstract terms. The conclusions they give are deliberately built in, and for this reason it is dangerous to consider them as a development of knowledge upon which further theoretical ideas can be based. On the other hand, they are not what economists traditionally call models, sets of more or less arbitrary assumptions that simulate reality. Their elements, the value of labour-power, the value of labour and the rate of surplus value are not suppositions, but actual elements of the capitalist economy expressed in general theoretical terms. Thus while abstract in the sense of not applying to any particular moment of capitalist history, and artificial in so far as the numerical values are contrived for simplicity, these schemata are not unrealistic, since the relations they express are the real relationships of capitalist production and its development. Thus it is not accidental that both schemata give ambiguous results about the movement in wages: in the case of increasing productivity, a rise in real wages and the value of labour is accompanied by a fall in the value of labour-power; with the intensification of labour real wages again go up and so does the value of labour-power, but the value of labour falls. The reason for this ambiguity originates in the complexity and ambiguity of the wage-form. If the wage was simply one thing, say the value of labour, it could only go up or down, and there would be no possibility of ambiguity. Thus the contradictory movements of the wage are, in one respect, nothing more than a quantitative expression of its diverse and complex nature. But in turn this diversity and complexity of the wage is, again in one respect, nothing more than a particular expression of the diverse and complex nature of the economic structure of which the wage is an integral part; in other words, an expression of the diverse and complex nature of capitalism itself. Telescoping this line of reasoning we can conclude that the contradictory movements among the different aspects of the wage are expressions of the contradictory nature of capitalism itself.

Once capitalism is firmly established upon the basis of the production of relative surplus value, the two strategies through which capital increases its rate of surplus value, increasing productivity and intensifying labour, bring about ambiguous movements in the movement of wages. In so far as capitalism is successful there must always be one aspect of the wage which falls and, to this extent, we can conclude that the development of capitalism involves the immiseration of labour. On the other hand, the possibilities exist for working class resistance and in the advanced capitalist countries, particularly since 1945, this has been successful in forcing up real wages. To this extent, we can conclude that the development of capitalism is consistent with improved working class living standards. Any characterisation of capitalist development from one point of view alone – as a process of immiseration or one of rising affluence – is inevitably one-sided and false. The search for a unilateral characterisation of capitalist development, however hedged around it might be with qualifications – growing affluence with as yet unrelieved pockets of poverty, or deepening poverty with the exception of a labour aristocracy – is understandable as an effort to find solid ground from which to judge it; but it is a naive undertaking quite inadequate to the problem. Simple moral judgements that capitalism is acceptable in so far as it creates affluence but unacceptable for generating poverty are abstract, necessarily indecisive, and quite beside the point. In dealing with a society where poverty and affluence are inseparably joined; where the production of wealth takes place on condition of the social or absolute poverty of the producers; mealy-mouthed morality must be eschewed in favour of a perspective of history and historical limits. But we have more details to cover before we can face up to this question.

3. NATURAL TIME AND THE TURNOVER OF CAPITAL

Suppose two capitals, A and B, identical in every respect but one – capital A completes its circuit twice as quickly as capital B. Ignoring constant capital whose presence would only complicate but not change this part of the analysis in any fundamental way, assume the two capitals both go into business with £1 million, all variable capital used to buy labour-power, and enjoy a rate of surplus value of 100 per cent. At the completion of the circuit $M - C^L_{MP} \ldots P \ldots C' - M'$ both capitals recover their original outlays together with an additional £1 million of surplus value. Only capital *A* achieves this in six months whereas capital *B* takes a year. The completion of a circuit, the movement from money-capital back to money-capital, is called a *turnover*, and the time it takes is called the *period of turnover*. Thus our two capitals are identical in every respect except the period of turnover – six months for *A* and a year for *B* – and what we must discover are the effects of this difference.

In our analysis so far we have been concerned with surplus value as such, and examined capitalist strategy as a means of maximising it. Now we must explore what capital can do over and above this, to speed up the momentum of its accumulation. In comparing two capitals we therefore assume the rate of surplus value to be constant, or to be precise we assume the *real rate of surplus value* constant. This real rate is the rate of surplus value as we know it, the ratio of paid to unpaid labour, the rate of exploitation. Thus both capital *A* and capital *B* exploit their workers at the rate of 100 per cent, paying them a value for their labour-power which equals only one half of the value they produce. At the end of each turnover both capitals acquire the same amount of surplus value, but at the end of the year capital *A*, which has completed two turnovers where capital *B* has managed only one, has twice as much surplus value. In other words, two capitals have the same real rate of surplus value but different *annual rates of surplus value*. Although it exploits labour at the same rate as capital *B*, capital *A* acquires surplus value twice as fast. For capital *B* the real and annual rates of surplus value are both equal to 100 per cent; for capital *A* the real rate of surplus value is also 100 per cent, but the annual rate is 200 per cent. What accounts for this difference, and is it consistent with the law of value as we have understood it so far?

Capital *B* presents no problems: in the course of a year £1 million is used to purchase labour-power, while the workers produce an output which has a value of £2 million, giving a real rate of surplus value of 100 per cent, and this is also the rate of surplus value per annum. At first sight capital *A* appears no different and the discrepancy between its two rates of surplus value seem to be due simply to accounting procedures. In each turnover £1 million is used to purchase labour-power and each realises a value of £2 million giving a surplus value of £1 million. In the course of a year when there are two turnovers, £2 million is used to purchase labour-power, £2 million of surplus value is produced, giving a rate of surplus value of 100 per cent. Whether we call this the real or the annual rate of surplus value seems immaterial since there is only one figure, and it is the same as that for capital *B*. This appears to confirm the view that if two capitals exploit labour at the same rate they must have equal rates of surplus value per unit of time, since time is merely a neutral yardstick against which the rate of surplus value is measured. But the practical capitalist knows better: for him time is not neutral at all – on the contrary time is money.

Consider capital A more closely. At the beginning of the year £1 million is advanced to purchase labour-power and at the end of six months, when the first turnover is complete, this sum returns together with £1 million surplus value. Now let us put this surplus value on one side for the moment and assume no immediate attempt is made to increase the scale of operations. At the beginning of the second half of the year a new circuit begins and a further £1 million is used to purchase labour-power. But the money that financed the first circuit is available and for this no new capital is required. In the course of the year capital A has to advance £2 million to get its surplus value of £2 million but this is done by using £1 million twice. Although from an accounting point of view £2 million used, from an economic point of view this is not the case, and in calculating the annual rate of surplus value only £1 million of this counts. In practical terms this point is easy to appreciate. To conduct one year's business and acquire a surplus value of £1 million, capital B requires £1 million. During the same period capital A acquires a surplus value of £2 million, but it too only needs £1 million in ready cash. Both capitals start the year by advancing the same sum, the only difference being capital A gets it back midway through the year and advances it again.

Parallel to the distinction between the real and the annual rate of surplus value we must note another between *capital employed* and *capital advanced*. Capital employed is the amount actually injected into the productive process: here where we ignore constant capital, it is the amount actually used as variable capital to purchase labour-power. Thus in the course of a year capital B employs £1 million. Capital A, on the other hand, which completes two turnovers in the twelve month period, employs £2 million. Capital advanced is the amount of money capital laid out, the amount of money required to maintain the momentum of a business; or, to look at it another way, the amount of money a firm must have in hand to start and maintain its operations. To keep going for a year capital B needs £1 million in hand, and this is the sum of capital it advances. But capital A, although it employs twice as much as capital B, can finance its larger operation with the same out of pocket expenses, being able to fund the second half of the year with the receipts of the first. This distinction between capital employed and capital advanced makes the difference between the real and annual rates of surplus value clear and highlights the importance of the rate of turnover. Thus:

Wages

$$\text{the real rate of surplus value (rs')} = \frac{\text{total annual surplus value (s)}}{\text{capital employed (ke)}}$$

$$\text{the annual rate of surplus value (as')} = \frac{\text{total annual surplus value (s)}}{\text{capital advanced (ka)}}$$

For capital B:

surplus value = £1 million; capital employed = £1 million so the real rate of surplus value = 100 per cent

as capital advanced equals capital employed, the annual rate of surplus value also equals 100 per cent.

For Capital A:

surplus value = £2 million capital employed = £2 million therefore the real rate of surplus value = 100 per cent.

But since capital advanced = £1 million the annual rate of surplus value = 200 per cent.

Thus on the basis of the same rate of exploitation capital *A* achieves an annual rate of surplus value double that of capital *B* because for each pound of surplus value acquired it advances only half the amount of capital. To understand why capital *A* is more successful than capital *B*, why the annual rate of surplus value is the critical indicator of capitalist success, we need only recall that the general criterion of capitalist success is accumulation, and that accumulation takes place in time. At the end of the year capital *B* has £2 million where it had only £1 million at the beginning, so that it can double the scale of its business, or accumulate at the rate of 100 per cent per annum. Capital *A* can do better: it has £3 million and so is able to accumulate at 200 per cent. In fact, it can do even better, for we assumed that it left the £1 million surplus value acquired halfway through the year idle, and there is no reason why it should. With this money it can start a new plant after six months, which brings in a further £1 million surplus value at the end of the year, making a total surplus value of £3 million that allows a rate of accumulation of 300 per cent. However, beyond noting that the advantages of a higher rate of surplus value are cumulative, and even greater than they appear at first sight, we will keep to the more straightforward case and assume that surplus value is only reinvested as new capital at the end of the year. In this case, the rate of accumulation equals the annual rate of surplus value and, for this reason, the annual rate is more critical to capital than the real rate.

Using the symbols from the definitions of the real and annual rates of surplus value with the addition of t which represents the number of turnovers completed in a year, we get the following:

$$\frac{as'}{rs'} = \frac{s}{ka} \times \frac{s}{ke}$$

$$= \frac{ka}{ke}$$

But:

$$ke = ka.t$$

Hence:

$$\frac{as'}{rs'} = \frac{ka}{ka.t}$$

$$= \frac{1}{t}$$

This states that the ratio of the annual rate of surplus value to the real rate equals the reciprocal of the number of turnovers per annum; or to put it more simply, the greater the number of turnovers a capital manages during a year, the higher its annual rate of surplus value in relation to its real rate. As capital aims to maximise its rate of accumulation, it follows that not only does it pursue strategies to maximise its real rate of surplus value, but that it also attempts to cut its turnover period down to a minimum.

So far we have examined capitalist strategy only from the point of view of the real rate of surplus value but all its initiatives have an additional temporal perspective which aim to reduce turnover time in order to accelerate accumulation. The imperatives of the *time-economy* are clearly visible from the beginning of industrial capitalism. The lengthening of the working day, and the introduction of the shift system that keeps plants running for twenty-four hours, may have more immediate explanations, such as efforts to increase the real rate of surplus value, or in the case of some processes that have to keep running continuously, they may be technically necessary. But in addition, it must be remembered any increase in the amount of work done during a day reduces the period of turnover and increases the annual rate of surplus value accordingly. Improvements in transport also play their part and apart from cutting costs, increasing productivity and making other contributions to the real rate of exploitation, the speeding up of getting goods to market also reduces turnover time. With the construction of a modern system of world transport, and the gradual reduction of the working day towards a norm of 8 hours, the emphasis shifted towards speeding up the process of production itself. The introduction of machinery at the beginning of the nineteenth century laid the foundations for intensification, but the conscious systematisation by capital of methods to dictate the pace and rhythm of work came later towards the end of the century with the development of 'scientific management' and 'work-study'. But it has been in the twentieth century with the development of machine systems, particularly conveyor-belt methods of production, that the most deliberate and conscious effort has been made to reduce turnover time by regulating the pace of work and generally intensifying labour. 'In my factory,' said Henry Ford, who initiated mass line production, 'the man must have every second necessary, but not a single unnecessary second.'

To appreciate the social significance of this assault on time we must think in terms of what, for convenience, we call *natural time*. In the light of work done by philosophers and physicists on the subject, this is a crude notion, and even social scientists could reasonably object that there is no absolute measure of time in the social world as it means different things in different societies. The development of artificial lighting has changed the balance between day and night; urbanisation with all it entails makes the seasons of the year less important than they were; improved medicine has altered the meaning of old age, while compulsory education and the abolition of child-labour has changed the significance and duration of childhood. Nevertheless there is a real sense, however tenuous, in which men have their own concept of time given by their own physiology and the nature of the world they inhabit. And while this might not be quite so precise and natural as it appears at first sight, it stands in sharp opposition to *capitalist time*, which is simply the period of turnover. As the reduction of this period increases the possible rate of accumulation, capital would ideally reduce it to zero and abolish time altogether. The pursuit of such an impossibility, a pursuit given by the nature of capital, is further evidence of its 'anti-humanity' and, in this sense, its irrationality. But considerations of humanity do not prevent it from making every practical effort it can to cut turnover periods to a minimum. The pollution of the physical environment and the corruption of the social milieu in the interests of what is euphemistically called economic growth are now commonplace; what is less clear is the abuse of natural time by capitalist time. The colonisation of time by capital threatens one of the foundations of human existence. It pervades every area of social life, though here we can only examine one of its aspects which is germane to the subject of this chapter – the effect of increased rates of turnover on wages and the working class standard of living.

In any catalogue of capitalist developments, the substantial increase in real wages involving not only a growth in the amount of goods consumed but a widening of the range, must occupy a prominent place. And behind it, the practice that has made it possible – the application of techniques of mass production which increase the productivity and intensity of labour. In other words, the methods of production that have made possible the spectacular rise in working-class living standards are precisely those that have played the decisive role in forcing up the real rate of surplus value. So much we have already considered together with the ambiguities it poses with respect to judging the ways, if any, that the working class can be said to have benefitted from capitalist development. We must now broach the same problem from the point of view of the annual rate of surplus value.

At first sight, it would seem that any increase in the annual rate of surplus value achieved exclusively through a reduction in the period of turnover can, at least, do the working class no harm in so far as the real rate of exploitation is unchanged. The workers employed by capital A are no worse off than those of capital B in so far as they are exploited at the same real rate of 100 per cent. In point of fact, this is unlikely to happen and capital A would in all probability take advantage of the situation and pay its workers the same amount per annum as capital B. But for the sake of argument suppose it pays them twice as much. On the other hand, if the intensity of working for capital A is double that of working for capital B, they perform twice as much labour to get this higher wage and, from the point of view of the value of labour, they are no better off. But this is a problem we have already looked into and there is nothing we can add. What we must consider here is the nature of the higher real wage that comes about when turnover is accelerated and ask whether even this is quite the clear-cut gain to the working class that it appears at first sight.

The first effect of a rise in real wages is obviously an increase in the level of working-class consumption. Once real wages have reached a level where the basic requirements of food and shelter are satisfied, any further increase takes the form of elaboration – more sophisticated basic products and entirely new ones. And it is at this point that the ambiguity creeps in. If every increase in real wages meant superior or more sophisticated products, or entirely new ones, a clear improvement in working-class living standards would take place. But all too often this is not the case. Rather there is a tendency for the period of consumption of a product to fall with its period of production, leaving the worker very much as he was. Suppose the turnover period of the capital producing shoes were reduced to a quarter; other things being equal, four times as many shoes would be produced as previously; and where the worker previously bought only one pair a year he could now buy four. But if the durability of shoes falls in the same proportion, there is a real sense in which he is no better off. The man who buys a new car every five years is hardly twice as well off as another who buys a new one every ten years, if the first car wears out after five years and the useful life of the second is twice as long. We refer here to the well-known phenomenon of accelerated depreciation, to the foreshortening of the life of products, whether due to physical reasons or the dictates of fashion. We wish to stress the points: first, that increases in working-class living standards measured by a greater volume of consumption must be offset by the extent to which the quality and durability of products has fallen; and second, that accelerated depreciation is a natural outcome of the drive by capital to increase its rate of accumulation by reducing its period of turnover. It would be pointless to deny that real gains have been made in living standards, particularly in the period since the end of the Second World War; equally it would be pointless to deny that a considerable part of consumer expenditure, especially on mass produced products, is a replacement demand that maintains rather than increases the standard of living. Thus even apparently clear working-class gains have their ambiguities, and there is no situation in which capital ever makes an open concession to the class it exploits.

4. THE VALUE OF LABOUR-POWER

Finally, we must return to the value of labour-power. This forms the basis of the analysis of the wage, but so far we have given it only a brief definition as the value of the commodities necessary for the worker to work. If we adjust this definition to treat the value of all labour-power we can avoid a few unnecessary complications by defining it as the value of all those commodities necessary to sustain the working class through time as a producing class and see that the commodities to be counted include those required for the sustenance not only of those members of the class who actually go out to work for a wage but dependents as well, children, old persons, and non-wage-earning wives. In determining the value of labour-power we should also include commodities consumed by members of the working class but paid for with money that is not earned as wages – unemployment benefits, social security payments and old-age pensions. Thus if we approach the concept of the value of labour-power from the point of view of the working class, rather than from the point of view of the individual worker, we get a more complete understanding of what it means. But we are still left with the problem we must consider here: what commodities count as necessary in this context? If we define necessary in narrow terms as what is biologically necessary, we would be forced to admit that the concept of the value of labour-power is of little use in understanding the level of wages, certainly in the advanced capitalist societies in the twentieth century. For many commodities that now form an established part of working-class consumption – cars, televisions, refrigerators, etc. – can hardly be considered indispensable. On the other hand, if we take a broader definition and talk of socially necessary consumption, we avoid this difficulty but run into another hardly less serious. For to argue that the products the working class consumes are by definition necessary in a social sense, because they are bought out of wages, is either a blunt assertion that does not further our analysis, or a reversal of the order of things. That is to say, it makes the definition of necessary consumption and the value of labour-power dependent upon wages in a way that gives no indication of how wages themselves are determined.

Although the definition of necessary consumption must include commodities that are biologically necessary to sustain the working class, clearly any definition of the value of labour-power that restricts itself in this way must be discounted. This requires us to develop the concept of the value of labour-power around a definition of socially necessary consumption and ask openly what socially necessary means in this context, and answer the question in a way that indicates how it changes from one period to the next with the accumulation of capital.

To do this we must introduce a second function of the wage which we have not mentioned so far. Since the products consumed by the working class are commodities produced by capital under the same conditions as all other commodities in order to make surplus value, the wage plays an integral part in the circulation of capital. Although value and surplus value originate in the sphere of production, they do not come fully into existence until the commodities in which they are embodied are sold for money – i.e. realised in circulation – and for many commodities, the possessor of the money which realises this value is the working class with its pay packet. Put it another way; if the workers did not spend their wages on commodities, many firms in the economy making up a considerable proportion of total capital, would be unable to sell their output and realise the value and surplus value tied up in it. The survival of capitalism as a system of social production depends as much upon this, as upon the continuous reproduction of the working class. In other words, when we search for the definition of necessary working-class consumption as the basis for the definition of the value of labour-power, we must take account not only of those commodities necessary to maintain the workers and their dependents at some morally acceptable level, but also that level of consumption, i.e. working class spending, that is necessary to realise the capital advanced in the wage-goods sector plus surplus value.

In fact, with the development of production and the growth in the mass of output this second function of the wage plays an increasingly important role in determining the value of labour-power. The elaboration of production in the wage-goods sector, and the mass production of consumer durables which has played such a central role in the accumulation process in the twentieth century, could never have occurred on the scale it has without an increase in real wages. Rising real wages, which we have seen are quite consistent with increasing rates of surplus value, have been indispensable for capitalist expansion, and in this respect we can say that the greater mass of commodities consumed by workers form a part of necessary consumption and therefore enter into the value of labour-power. In other words, once account is taken of the second function of the wage as a medium of circulating capital, the concept of necessary consumption acquires an additional dimension: necessary consumption is no longer simply that consumption necessary to sustain the working class but also that consumption that is necessary for the production of capital. For this reason the level of necessary consumption and the value of labour-power is not only determined by the needs of the working class, it is also a function of capitalist development which changes its scale and pattern with the accumulation of capital.

Like everything else in capitalist society the importance of working class consumption is not without its ambiguities. Formally speaking, its importance as a medium of realising capital and surplus value in the wage-goods industries cannot be denied; and its growing importance with the development of mass production in the twentieth century is practically demonstrated by the growth of advertising. In the nineteenth century with low levels of consumption, the function of wages to circulate capital required little direct management as animal needs were sufficient to ensure the expenditure of money-wages. At the same time, the pattern of demand was easy to anticipate, since a large proportion of working class income was inevitably used to purchase rudimentary necessities. But the growth in real wages has made working class demand more problematic: it is one thing to predict the demand for bread; quite another to predict, and anticipate with large initial advances of capital, the demand for cars. But while the accumulation of capital is more than ever dependent upon the growth of working class consumption – hence the development of demand management in all its aspects – it would be wrong to conclude that capital has an unqualified interest in rising wages. For it is as true today as it ever was that the pursuit of maximum surplus value is the first concern of capital, and that any increase, in any aspect, of the wage lowers the rate of surplus value below what it might otherwise be.

In relation to the working class, capital is both a buyer and seller – buying labour-power from it at one moment of its circuit and selling it commodities at another. But the sum that capital pays out as buyer, a sum it naturally wishes to minimise, determines the size of the market which, as a seller, it wishes to maximise. The possibilities of disjuncture here are legion and the economists' notion of the 'equilibrium wage' which balances conflicting requirements is nothing more than a chimera. The recurrence of periodic crises can be traced back to this point – the near practical impossibility of the capitalist economy achieving the level of wages which concedes the maximum rate of surplus value on the one side, and realises the capital advanced in wage-good production plus surplus value on the other. In more general terms it is clear that while capital as a whole has conflicting interests in the level of wages, the particular interests of individual capitals vary with their situation in the productive circuit. Thus those firms mass-producing consumer durables tend to adopt a more liberal attitude to wages than other firms that manufacture means of production. In some quarters the conflict between different sections of capital is seen as the most important expression of the fundamental incongruities of capitalist production. But without denying the presence and importance of inter-capitalist conflicts of interest, it must always be remembered that every capital has a general interest that stands in opposition to that of the working class. In the case of wage determination this is particularly apparent. If the problem of determining an equilibrium wage, which reconciles the interests of capital as buyer and seller, were merely a question of reconciling the interests of different capitals, it would simply be a technical problem and relatively easy to solve. But the wage question involves the working class; hence it is a political problem that arises from the class nature of capitalist society and, as such, has no permanent or final solution.

5. WAGES STRUGGLE

In our analysis of co-operation and machine production, we saw that working class participation could not be guaranteed and that a problem of control exists for capital. Again in the analysis of the wage-form, whereby labour-power, unlike any other commodity, is paid for only after its use-value has been realised, it again became clear that capital cannot take the working class for granted. But generally speaking we have tended to treat the working class as the passive premise of capitalist production, as a class to which things happen. We must now correct this impression. It is one thing to say that in capitalist society power and initiative rest with capital which controls the means of production and directs accumulation, technology and output; it is another to claim that in the face of this power the working class is helpless or at best defensive. On the contrary, the working class continuously resists capitalist power as a condition of its existence, sometimes more forcibly than others, sometimes more successfully than others; but though the intensity of the working class struggle varies it is always present as a permanent feature of capitalist reality. Nowhere is this more evident than in the field of wages.

In our analysis of the effects of increases in the productivity and intensity of labour, we have seen how capital can concede increased real wages without suffering any drop in the rate of surplus value. To this we can add the observation that the concession of higher wages is more than a sop to labour in appeasement for higher rates of exploitation, but a measure that is necessary for maintaining the momentum of accumulation. Nevertheless it does not follow that capital willingly concedes wage increases since its short-term interests, as well as the interests of individual firms, always lay in the direction of holding wages down. On the other hand, no such conflict of interests affects the working class, and this is the telling factor in the situation. To the extent that it is able to organise itself in pursuit of its economic interests, the working class plays a decisive role in breaking the impasse among the various interests and fractions of capital and imposing upon capital as an external necessity the upward movement of wages that accumulation on a social scale requires. In other words, the working class struggle against capital for higher wages breaks through the immediate short-term and individual interests of capital: by its opposition to capital, the working class brings about the conditions necessary for maintaining the momentum of accumulation. Thus the short answer to the question – what process determines the level of socially necessary consumption and the value of labour-power? – is the class struggle. A more complete answer situates the class struggle within the general development of production, the value of commodities, the pattern of output and the type of techniques employed. But the fact remains that the value of labour-power is not determined by economic forces defined in the narrow sense: there are no market laws to be discovered that stipulate the level of necessary consumption; no strict correlation between wages and the technical conditions of production. If the theory of the value of labour-power is indeterminate from this point of view, if it is an economic theory that drifts untidily into the sphere of politics, this is because the capitalist world itself is indeterminate and no amount of elegant and precise economic reasoning will ever make it tidy.

The introduction of the class struggle at this point in the admittedly restricted guise of the wage struggle may appear as little more than an expedient to get the theory of value round an awkward corner. The critic who points out that the value of labour-power and its correlative, the rate of surplus value, are the crucial variables of the theory of value but cannot be explained as determinate magnitudes within the framework of this theory without recourse to external factors such as the class struggle, the development of trade unions and the like, appears to hold solid ground. But in this instance, criticism of a theory for having to look outside its own field for the determination of variables that it puts at its very centre, holds no force. For the first aim of the theory of value is not to define in detail the forces that determine the magnitude of the value of labour-power and the rate of surplus value, but to establish these categories as such; to demonstrate in theoretical terms that the value of labour-power and the rate of surplus value are real categories of the capitalist political economy even though they are invisible in the forms through which political economy is immediately known. Furthermore, the class struggle, the relentless opposition of the working class to capital, is not an extraneous assumption plucked from nowhere to patch a hole in an economic theory; the class struggle is nothing but the concrete expression of the law of value; or, to put it the other way round, the law of value is the general theoretical statement of the class struggle.

When we move from such questions as what is the nature of labour-power and its value, and what is surplus value and the rate of surplus value?—that is when we move from questions of a qualitative nature to questions of a quantitative kind: what determines the magnitude of the value of labour-power and the rate of surplus value?—we are moving away from the general level at which the law of value begins, into a less abstract world. New and more appropriate concepts are required, though of course they must be consistent with those already in use. By analogy, a map of the world can help us locate a country, but to locate a town within that country we need a more detailed map; and to find a particular street, an even more detailed plan. To criticise a theory of value because it does not give us the precise determinations of the value of labour-power is akin to criticising a map of the world for not marking Oxford Street or Fifth Avenue.

7 Profits

From wages we turn to profits, the other category through which the value relations of capitalism make themselves known – or perhaps we should say unknown. For like wages, profits present these relations in a way that masks their nature. We have seen how this happens with the wage-form; how the value of labour-power appears as the value of labour and the knowledge of surplus value disappears behind the illusion that all labour is paid labour. Profit deepens the fog with which wages envelop exploitation. By relating it to total capital advanced, $\dfrac{s}{c+v}$, the rate of profit makes surplus value appear as much the product of the means of production bought with constant capital as of labour-power bought with variable capital. From here it is a short step to the conclusion that profit is the product of capital as such – a return to capital just as wages are a payment for labour. Orthodox economics, which takes wages and profits as self-evident categories, inevitably adopts this position; as one economist put it, exploitation is a noise rather than a noun.

This representation of surplus value as profit, and then as the return on capital, parallels the representation of the value of labour-power as the value of labour in another important respect. Like the wage-form, it is not a simple disguise that can be cast aside to reveal the true character behind, but a form of existence that is necessary and indispensible. The payment of wages as the value of labour serves a practical end, since the only way a capitalist can be sure of getting any work from his employees is by paying them afterwards and in proportion to the amount they do. The rate of profit has the equally practical function of determining the rate of accumulation. Assume a firm that advances £1 million, half as constant capital and half as variable capital, and enjoys a rate of surplus value of 100 per cent. The absolute amount of surplus value it gains at the end of the year, assuming a twelve month turnover period, is £0.5 million. It could, in principle, use this sum to double its labour force, but this would be a futile policy since there would be no funds available to supply the additional workers with the means of production which we must once again take into consideration. Its rational course of action is to expand its labour force by only 50 per cent, which costs £0.25 million, leaving another £0.25 million over to purchase the additional means of production that the extra workers require. In this case its rate of expansion is 50 per cent, a rate of expansion that equals its rate of profit: $\dfrac{£0.5 \text{ million } s}{£0.5 \text{ million } c + £0.5 \text{ million } v}$. Since it is the general rule that the rate of accumulation equals the rate of profit and not the rate of surplus value, it is readily understandable why the former figures so largely in practical analysis and the latter recedes into obscurity; although the rate of surplus value is the more critical of the ratios since it expresses class relationships directly. (We can add that a shortening of the period of turnover increases the annual rate of profit relative to the real rate, in the same way as it increases the annual rate of surplus value in relation to its real rate, and increases the rate of accumulation accordingly.)

The difference between the rate of profit and the rate of surplus value is that the former takes account of constant capital and the latter does not: $\dfrac{s}{c+v}$ as opposed to $\dfrac{s}{v}$. Alternatively, if we express the rate of profit as $\dfrac{s}{v} \div \left(1 + \dfrac{c}{v}\right)$ we can see that the rate of surplus value is one of its components. The other, which we have not yet examined, is the organic composition of capital, $\dfrac{c}{v}$, and it is to this we now turn our attention.

1. THE ORGANIC COMPOSITION OF CAPITAL

The organic composition of capital is the ratio of constant to variable capital: to be absolutely precise, it is the ratio of the value of capital advanced as constant capital to that advanced as variable capital. These values depend upon the actual amounts of various commodities purchased under these heads and their individual values. Thus:

$$c = k.\,ak$$

$$v = l.\,bl$$

where k is the mass of means of production; ak the value of each individual item; l the mass of labour-power purchased; bl the value of a unit of labour-power; and c and v have their usual meanings of constant and variable capital. Thus the organic composition of capital is really the product of two distinct variables:

$$\frac{c}{v} = \frac{k}{l} \times \frac{ak}{bl}$$

where $\frac{k}{l}$ can be defined as the *technical composition of capital*; and $\frac{ak}{bl}$ the *value composition of capital*.

To analyse how the organic composition of capital tends to change, it is therefore necessary to understand first how each of its constituents tends to move separately; and then how they move in relation to each other. As the value composition of capital presents less problems, we start with it first.

To be clear, the value composition of capital is the ratio of the *unit* value of two sets of commodities – commodities that serve as instruments and materials of production on the one side, and labour-power on the other. At the same time, we know that the value of a unit of labour-power resolves itself into the value of the commodities that the worker must consume to supply this labour-power; so that the ratio that counts is that between the average values of producer goods and of wage goods. Since both sets of commodities are produced under conditions that have become increasingly similar with the development of capitalism, it is not possible to find any systematic long-term tendency for this ratio to move in one direction rather than the other. In the first part of the nineteenth century it was generally thought that a long-term rise in the value of wage goods was inevitable, because the greater part of working class consumption consisted of food and special conditions were believed to be attached to agricultural production. As the expansion of agriculture approached the margin of cultivatable land, the quality of land was expected to fall and the value of produce to rise, since any given amount of labour produces less output on poor land. It is now commonplace to point out, with hindsight, how the cultivation of vast new territories outside Europe, and improved methods of cultivation, prevented this law of diminishing returns asserting itself. Colonial exploitation also made significant contributions to the supply of cheap foodstuffs. But of particular importance, especially in the twentieth century, has been the diversification of working class consumption, with the result that a substantial proportion of wage-goods are products of manufacturing industry. At the same time, it must be remembered that not all the means of production are machines and buildings: under this category must also be included materials of various sorts that are appropriated directly from nature and are subject to the same conditions and restraints that apply to agriculture. For all these reasons it appears impossible to discern any systematic tendency for the value of the one group of goods to vary significantly in relation to the other; and when analysing movements in the organic composition of capital, the only reasonable assumption is that the value composition of capital remains constant. It must be noted that this constancy applies only to the relative value of producer-goods and wage-goods, their values in relation to each other; not to their absolute values which fall with improvements in productivity.

The Technical Composition of Capital This is the ratio of means of production to labour-power as physical quantities. Since its elements are expressed in different units they are not readily reducible to a simple indicator. Nevertheless, there is a quantitative dimension to the relation between the masses of the means of production and labour-power even if there is no unit immediately at hand to express it. All the evidence suggests this ratio rises, and that workers handle a greater volume of materials and instruments of production, as capitalism develops and accumulation proceeds. The most impressionistic comparison of a nineteenth century factory with a contemporary one confirms the view that the technical composition of capital has grown considerably and recent evidence suggests this trend is continuing at what might be an accelerating pace. There are strong grounds for going beyond such observations and positing the tendency for the technical composition of capital to rise as a systematic and structural feature of accumulation and a necessary outcome of capitalist production itself.

These can be summarised under two heads corresponding to the division of the means of production into materials of labour on the one side, and instruments on the other. An increase in the volume of materials per unit of labour would appear as an inevitable outcome of a growth in production, itself a consequence of accumulation. Undoubtedly one of the results of technical progress is a reduction in the amount of raw materials used per unit of output. In the nineteenth century, to take one example, a steady reduction occurred in the amount of coal used to smelt a ton of iron; and in the twentieth century, to take another, the development of synthetics has achieved economies on an even more dramatic scale. General technical developments can save materials indirectly – contrast the smallness of electronic calculating machines with that of the bulky mechanical devices they have replaced. Notwithstanding these economies, the sheer growth in the volume of production has certainly increased the absolute mass of materials productively consumed, while increases in productivity and intensity have increased this mass more rapidly than labour-power. This is the first reason for insisting that a rise in the technical composition of capital is an inevitable feature of accumulation.

The second reason, or set of reasons, arises from the particular role played by the instruments of labour in capitalist production, which we have already considered in our analysis of machinery. Here the improvements in productivity that machines make possible, plus the greater degree of control they allow management over labour, are paramount. But it is possible to perceive an even more general tendency than this, whereby the natural development of capitalism is the progressive displacement of labour from production and its replacement by impersonal means of production. This development, as we shall see later, is ultimately inconsistent with the social relations of capitalism whose rationale is to impose work as a necessity upon the working class, but there are the most compelling practical reasons of cost effectiveness and competitive advantage for individual firms to pursue policies that make this development a reality. In general, it always pays a firm to replace living labour with machinery if this reduces its *cost-price of production* – i.e. the amount it advances as constant plus variable capital $(c+v)$ – for any given level of output. In this way the technical advantages of mechanisation in reducing necessary labour time, both living and past, give a systematic bias in favour of a rising technical organic composition of capital.

Suppose the average conditions of production in an industry made up of firms that produce more or less identical products, say refrigerators, is: $50c + 50v + 50s = 1$ refrigerator. On the assumption of equal exchange, which we have as yet no reason to change, and which in this context is only a convenient simplification, a refrigerator sells for £150. Of this sum, £100 is the cost price of production that must be met by the capitalist; £50 is surplus value; and the average rate of profit is 50 per cent. Now suppose one firm changes its methods of production, increasing its constant capital to 60 and reducing its variable capital to 30, giving it a new cost price for producing a single refrigerator of $90 - (60c + 30v)$. If the market price of refrigerators remains £150 the innovating firm realises an effective surplus value of 60, which gives a rate of profit of 66 per cent — $60s/60c + 60v$. But suppose the rate of surplus value for the new method remains 100 per cent; the new conditions of production are $60c + 30v + 30s = 120$. As more firms adopt the new methods the value of refrigerators falls to £120. Later we will deal with the implication of the fall in the average level of profit that innovation can bring about – from 50 per cent to 33 per cent in this case: but the point that counts here is that the short-term rate of profit for the individual firm increases from 50 per cent to 66 per cent, and that this is usually sufficient inducement for the leading firms to introduce new methods of production. Once a single firm has pioneered new cost-cutting technologies, other firms must follow suit or perish.

The tendency for the degree of mechanisation to rise in capitalist society is thus a consequence of two factors: one technical and one economic. The technical factor is that increased mechanisation, which changes the ratio of dead to living labour, reduces the total labour time necessary to produce any given output; the economic factor is that in capitalist society this reduction can always be used by an individual firm to increase its rate of profit – at least in the short period. In conjunction with the increased consumption of materials per unit of labour, this growth in the mechanisation of production adds up to a systematic tendency for the technical composition of capital to rise. Link this, in turn, to the constancy of the value composition and we are drawn to the conclusion that a rising organic composition of capital is an integral aspect of the process of accumulation. The reduction in the amount of labour relative to the means of production is not a contingency due to technical developments that occur autonomously; it is capitalist development, as such, which sponsors technical innovation on a hitherto unprecedented scale and then presses it into production in the search for increased profitability.

2. THE CONCENTRATION OF CAPITAL

The first effect of an increase in the organic composition of capital is an increase in the size of firms and a reduction in their number. In some cases this reduction is absolute; always it is relative to output. This is the *concentration of capital*. The economics of the process are straightforward revolving around the increase in the economic scale of production induced by mechanisation and the fact that this increase takes place more quickly than the growth of total output. The schema on p. 98 illustrates the point.

Effects of increases in the economic scale of production on the size of firms

Industrial output (index)	Economic output (index)	Number of firms
100	5	20
150	10	15
200	20	10
250	50	5
300	100	3

Economic output here means that level of production at which the average cost price of production is reduced to its minimum; this schema illustrates, in a stylised way, what happens as this level rises more quickly than industrial output – the number of firms falls and their size grows. This process is verified many times over in the development of major industries – cars, electronics, oil, chemicals – where the number of independent firms has declined steadily throughout this century until a mere handful dominate world production. Capitalist competition in reality, unlike the fantasy of the orthodox textbooks, where a large number of small firms are assumed to co-exist in an uneasy but permanent truce, is a battle in which there are winners and losers; where the winners get bigger and bigger and the losers disappear, or remain simply as vestigial brand names.

It is tempting to conclude that the concentration of capital is the natural outcome of competition, but this is not the case and accepting it as an explanation has implications that are seriously misleading. If there were no tendency for the scale of economic output to increase, individual firms would have no real inducement or possibility of expansion. In the illustration used a moment ago, we saw how an increase in the organic composition of capital can reduce the cost price of production, and concede to the firm which makes the innovation a higher rate of profit, so long as other firms continue to produce in the same way and the value of the commodity on the market remains unchanged. If no innovations occur, firms remain in balance with each other, and conditions approximating to what economists call 'the competitive equilibrium' prevail. (Incidentally it is worth noting that the economic theory of perfect competition is constructed on the assumption of a constant technology and rising costs which bar any firm from expanding – i.e. the orthodox theory of capitalism presupposes the absence of accumulation.) As soon as we acknowledge the possibility of a fall in the average cost price of production and make the reasonable assumption that this coincides with an increase in the scale of economic output, the competitive balance becomes highly unstable. Once a single firm has introduced new methods

Profits 99

of production and gains a higher than average rate of profit, it pays it to expand as far as possible. This expansion is facilitated by its ability to reduce its price and still gain a higher than average rate of profit. In our illustration we assumed that the initial value of a refrigerator was £150, the cost price of production was £100, and the average rate of profit 50 per cent. Since the new methods of production reduce the cost price to £90, the innovating firm can bring its price down to £135 and still earn the average rate of profit of 50 per cent. At a price, say, of £140 it can gain a higher than average rate of profit and undercut its competitors, who are immediately put under intense pressure. Some will respond and make the necessary adjustments to their methods of production; others for various reasons will not. One thing is clear, however: so long as the rise in scale of economic output is greater than the increase in total output the number of competing firms must fall.

From this we must conclude that the concentration of capital is a natural outcome of competition only when it occurs in conjunction with a rise in the organic composition of capital, which reduces the average cost price of production and increases economic output. But like so many conclusions this one immediately raises a new question, and a particularly important one: what is the relation between these two aspects of the concentration process – competition and the rise in the organic composition of capital? As the rise in the organic composition of capital is an integral part of the process of accumulation the question can be posed in even wider terms of the relationship between competition and the accumulation of capital. Its significance then becomes evident: as the nature of competition has changed so profoundly in the twentieth century with the monopolisation of large sectors of production and vast state intervention, the issue at stake concerns the nature of contemporary capitalism itself—whether indeed it is capitalism at all, or whether the decline of competition as it existed classically in the nineteenth century has ushered in some new type of post-capitalist society in which the questions of class and politics and the alternative of socialism are no longer relevant.

Since the concentration of capital has so far taken place through competition and rises in the organic composition of capital acting in conjunction with each other, there is no empirical evidence that allows us to sort out the relationship between them, and we must proceed theoretically. In this light it is plain that the only interpretation consistent with the over-all view of capitalism presented here is that the rise in the organic composition of capital takes precedence as the driving force, and that competition acts in a secondary role as the medium through which the general character of capitalism imposes itself upon individual firms. The drive to accumulate and increase the organic composition of capital finds its ultimate origins in the nature of capital itself, and the characteristic form of its circuit, $M - C - M'$. So long as the economic activity of one class of society conforms to this circuit, the drive to accumulate must be present. But in capitalist society the existence of a class that buys in order to sell implies the existence of another that sells in order to buy, and which has nothing to sell but its capacity to work. Hence the accumulation of capital and the tendency of its organic composition to grow, arise from the class structure of capitalist society itself, alongside which the division of capital into individual firms that compete with each other for profits and survival pales into secondary significance.

Having said this it would be wrong to underestimate the importance of competition as a means of reminding individual capitalists of their class duty to exploit labour and amass surplus value at the greatest possible rate. Contrary to the view that it is an expression of innate human nature, competition *depersonalises* the capitalist *qua* capitalist and reduces him to an individuated element of social capital. Consider the classic individual capitalist, the entrepreneurial hero of orthodox economics. From a juridical point of view the capital embodied in the firm is private property which he can dispose of as he wishes. In so far as capital is property and the capitalist a property owner, the individual is under no particular social pressure to do one thing or another. Apart from liquidating his assets, in which case he gives up all pretence of being a capitalist, he could, in principle, draw out all the surplus value the enterprise generates and use it exclusively for his private pleasure – i.e. he could decide to remain a capitalist but one who does not accumulate capital. But it is precisely this choice that competition denies him, except perhaps for a short period and in special circumstances. For unless all capitalists agree to a strategy of non-accumulation, any individual capitalist who decides to follow his bent and eschew accumulation would soon find his profits reduced, as his rivals introduce new methods of production that undercut him on the market. Hence to survive as a capitalist, as opposed to a mere property owner, the individual has no choice but to compete, and there is no way he can do this except by turning substantial parts of his surplus value into new capital – in a word, by accumulating. Since *laissez faire* was first celebrated some two hundred years ago by Adam Smith who saw the 'free market' and open competition as an 'invisible hand that leads men to achieve an end that is no part of their intention', competition has acted as an objective constraint upon those property owners whose property is capital. In other words, competition determines the action of capitalists as capitalists, reducing the individual capitalist to a mere personal representative of capital, depersonalising him into the functioning agent of a social relation of production which is none of his making. The fact that this determination – the negation of personal individuality – presents itself in the opposite guise as a condition of individual freedom, and moreover, makes the accumulation of capital appear the result of choices freely taken by individuals in competition with each other, is yet a further example of the fetishism that pervades capitalist society. We can add that the way in which competition reduces individuals into the representatives of capital by appealing to the twin atavisms of fear and greed has stamped an indelible mark upon bourgeois culture, and contributed in full measure to making capitalist society as uncivilised as it is.

As the process of accumulation proceeds, the importance of competition declines, not only because larger firms can influence the market and collude with their rivals more easily, but because the object of competition, the individual entrepreneur, becomes an increasingly marginal figure. With the concentration of capital, the function of competition to depersonalise the individual capitalist diminishes steadily as depersonalisation occurs immediately within the confines of the enterprise itself. We refer here to the multiple ownership of companies, the separation of ownership from control and the emergence of a professional managerial caste: developments which in some quarters are seen as the economic conditions of post-capitalist society, but which, on the contrary, constitute a higher development of capitalist organisation to deal with the growth of production and the development of new methods of exploitation.

Whether one should go as far as referring to this managerial caste as the capitalist class is a moot point. To the extent that it does not participate in the ownership of capital is has little in common with the entrepreneurial bourgeoisie it has superseded; while its dependence upon wage-labour gives it a formal economic station in life akin to that of the working class. On the other hand, it is this caste that represents capital in production and organises the exploitation of the working class. And although its income is not directly geared to surplus value in the same way as that of the old class of entrepreneurs, its economic fate is linked to the success of the various enterprises that employ it, and this success is determined in terms of profit and accumulation. We can add that the decline of competition has been matched by the growing importance of banking capital which lends money to industrial enterprises and deducts part of the surplus value they produce in the form of interest. The circuit of banking capital is the circuit of capital stripped down to its most essential form, $M - M'$, and this leaves no room for doubt about the purpose of its business. If the interaction of rival capitalists in the market is no longer sufficient to keep firms in line, the power of the banks to make money available, or deny it, certainly is. Needless to say the criterion that concerns a bank most when making a loan to an enterprise is profitability, and while it would be going too far to say that the banks have superseded the competitive market as the medium through which the laws of social capital are imposed as immanent necessities on individual firms, their activities certainly make good any shortcomings that the decline of competition has left in this field.

The modern corporation with its bureaucracy of hired managerial cadres is the characteristic representative of capital when concentration has reached its present level. The emergence of what is commonly called monopoly capitalism has severed the link between private individual property and capital that was characteristic of an earlier phase of development; and the managerial caste which this development has engendered represents the interests of capital just as efficiently as the old bourgeoisie – perhaps even more completely. Lacking the possibility of transforming capital into private property for consumption and with no alternative to advancing the interests of capital but a slide into complete proletarian status, the managerial caste is finely attuned to the requirements of accumulation. A product of capitalist society with no perspectives beyond its narrow horizons; vocationally trained in ways that make even the conception of alternatives impossible; totally dependent upon capital for its prestige and status; the managerial caste pursues the process of accumulation with a zeal and commitment that few captains of industry could rival. Its dependence upon wages underlines its dependence upon capital and keeps it in line; just as competition controlled the independent entrepreneur of the nineteenth century and the private capitalists who still operate in the interstices of the corporation-dominated economy today. When the vast bulk of capital is the private property of individuals, it appears that in this relation of property the owner is the subject and the capital the object. But this appearance like all others is deceptive: the capitalist owns capital in a juridical sense; in an economic sense it is capital that owns the capitalist. The emergence of the managerial caste is a further development of the depersonalisation of the capitalist brought about by competition and of his reduction to being merely the representative of capital. It would be an exaggeration to claim that the private ownership of capital which left the capitalist class a margin of autonomy vis-à-vis capital, has been completely overcome by the collective ownership of the joint stock company, and that the day-to-day control of capital has passed entirely into the hands of the managerial caste. Elements of the old form remain and combine with the new. Moreover they coexist in relative harmony, for no fundamental differences exist between them in so far as each represents the economic requirements of capital as an impersonal social force. Thus the erosion of the traditional forms of private property and competition does not spell the end of capitalism as some commentators claim, only the end of a particular phase in its development. The emergence this century of the modern corporation, directed by a mangerial caste with little or no direct ownership, continues the process of depersonalisation in new and equally effective ways; continues the rule of capital and constitutes much less of a rupture with the past than the advocates of the *new industrial state* or the *mixed economy* believe.

Finally, in this context, we must consider the proletarianisation of the representatives of capital which is often cited as evidence of the disappearance of the working class as a distinct social entity. At first sight it appears possible to define the working class simply in terms of wage-labour, but then the difficulty arises of the many 'wage-workers' like professional managers whose social situation differs fundamentally from that of the working class in everything except their form of remuneration. This has encouraged a trend in modern sociology to deny the applicability of the old class categories altogether; and to argue that in place of the division of society into capitalist class and working class there now exists a range of interest groups – manual workers, clerical workers, professionals of various kinds, managers and so on – which merge into each other. If everybody today is a wage-earner, then everybody is a worker, and though differences might exist as regards income, there is no more fundamental division than this. This simplifies the point but the question is clear: if the managers of capital are as dependent upon wages as other employees, how can one make a sharp distinction between the two groups in economic terms and define them as classes with opposed and incompatible interests? If this question appears to have none but the obvious answer we can confront it with another equally disarming question: given the fact that profit still exists as a category, what other source can this profit have but the exploitation of living labour in the process of production, controlled by these wage-earning managers in the name of the corporations which appropriate this profit? The plain fact is that the distinct existence of the working class producing surplus value is unaffected by the *proletarianisation* of the managers of capital; or to put it the other way round, the proletarianisation of the managers of capital does not make them part of the working class so long as their economic practice is the organisation of production on a capitalist basis whose result is surplus value.

But although the proletarianisation of management does nothing to change the fundamental relations of capitalist production, it does reveal features of these relations that were hidden in earlier epochs when the opposition in society presented itself in terms of the poverty and exploitation of the working class on the one side, and the independent wealth of the capitalist class on the other. Now it is clear that capitalism produces poverty on both sides of the class divide; that the managers of capital are no more in control of their economic conditions than workers. Corporate capitalism does not abolish the fundamental division of society into the working and capitalist classes, what it does is homogenise the economic and social conditions, creating a dull uniformity of life which embraces both classes. Sometimes mistaken for socialism, this tendency is the very opposite – the socialisation of misery. The old bourgeois nightmare of communism as a uniform society that admits no individuality has nothing to do with communism as a yet untried experience, but everything to do with the evolving reality of late capitalism, where the regime of capital replaces its former mediations and submerges both ruled and rulers into mediocrity.

3. SOCIAL CAPITAL AND THE AVERAGE RATE OF PROFIT

We must now examine in more exact economic detail how individual capitals relate to each other, and how social capital imprints its character on individual capitals through this relationship. As this relationship is realised through the buying and selling of commodities, and large monopolistic corporations produce and trade commodities no differently from the one-man business they have superseded, it is a general feature of capitalist production, unchanged in any fundamental way by the concentration of capital and its consequences. Its analysis concerns the *transformation of values into prices of production*; which has become a popular intellectual pastime in some quarters. Here we are interested in what has become known as the *transformation problem* only in so far as it is crucial to understanding inter-capitalist relationships and the nature of social capital.

Assume the economy is made up of two industries: this is purely for

Profits

convenience, and we could as well assume five or fifty industries. Further assume that the output of both industries is essential for the reproduction of the economy – this is the case where one industry produces wage-goods and the other the means of production. In this situation, an individual firm finds itself in direct competition with the other firms in its own industry and in some form of indirect relationship to firms in the other industry. It is the second relationship, the indirect one, that concerns us here, but a few words are necessary on the first.

We have seen that within a single industry firms operate with different methods of production – i.e. different organic compositions of capital – and gain different rates of profit. At any moment in time when the value of the commodity tends towards the average, efficient firms have a lower than average cost price of production and make a higher than average rate of profit. And, as we saw, it is this inverse variation of the rate of profit with the cost price of production that induces firms to cut costs and search for new methods of production which lead in the end to the concentration of capital. For the moment, however, we are concerned with the structure of the economy, the interrelationship of its parts, and these are best studied outside the process of accumulation. For this reason, we abstract from conditions within a single industry and treat the firms that comprise it as though they were a single unit producing under average conditions and earning the average rate of profit. Such a procedure, it must be stressed, does not deny variations in the rate of profit among firms in the same industry; it simply puts these variations to one side so that the conditions determining the relationship between firms in different industries that do not compete directly with each other can be brought to the fore.

Thus, we have a situation where there are two industries made up of firms all earning the appropriate average rate of profit. The next question concerns the relationship between these average profit rates: will the average rate of profit in industry (1) equal the average rate of profit in industry (2), or not? The answer would appear to depend upon the conditions of production prevailing in the industries. Thus if:

$$100c + 50v + 50s = 200o \qquad (1)$$

and
$$100c + 50v + 50s = 200o \qquad (2)$$

both industries gain the same rate of profit since they have identical conditions of production. The two components of the rate of profit, the organic composition of capital and the rate of surplus value are the same in both cases. The following conditions also yield equal rates of profit, although they are not identical:

$$100c + 50v + 50s = 200o \tag{1}$$

$$75c + 75v + 50s = 200o \tag{2}$$

The organic composition of capital is higher in industry (1) ($100c/50v$) than in industry (2) ($75c/75v$), but the rate of surplus value is also higher in industry (1) ($50s/50v$ as opposed to $50s/75v$) and these differences balance each other out to give a rate of profit of 33 per cent in both industries. It is, of course, possible that this happens in practice, even that the industries are identical, but it is highly improbable and there are no solid grounds for assuming that the conditions of production systematically create an equal rate of profit across different industries. Even if we assume the rate of surplus value to be the same in each industry, not an altogether plausible assumption but a convenient one, variations in the organic composition of capital alone would lead to different rates of profit. Thus:

$$100c + 50v + 50s = 200o \tag{1}$$

$$75c + 75v + 75s = 225o \tag{2}$$

Here the rate of surplus value in both industries equals 100 per cent, but the organic composition of capital differs, with the result that the rate of profit is 33 per cent in industry (1) but 50 per cent in industry (2). We could allow the rates of surplus value also to vary between the industries and still get different rates of profit, but this would add little of interest to this part of the analysis: hence we take this example as a statement of the general case. Thus in answer to the question are the average rates of profit of different industries equal to each other, the answer must be no. There is no reason why conditions of production in different industries should in general lead to the same rate of profit in the short period; nor is there any feature of the process of accumulation that achieves a balance between industries, through time permitting us to treat variations in industrial rates of profit as temporary phenomena, that are ironed out taking one year with the next.

On the other hand, there are compelling economic reasons why the same average rate of profit should prevail throughout the economy, since the capitalist economy could not function without a mechanism which brought a *general* or *social* rate of profit. The explanation for this is straightforward enough. If capital in industry (1) systematically earns a lower rate of profit than capital in industry (2) there will be a movement of investment out of (1) and into (2). But unless this movement leads to a change in the conditions of production, and there is no reason why it should, the result will be that sooner or later industry (1) is completely run down and only industry (2) remains. But this result is impossible for two reasons:

1. The output of industry (1) is essential for the reproduction of the economy. If we assume that industry (1) produces means of production and industry (2) wage-goods, then the economy would cease to function as industry (1) closed down since the elements of constant capital used up in production could not be replaced. If the situation were reversed, and industry (2) closed down, the breakdown would be just as complete, since there would be no products to sustain the workers. In other words, the imperatives of basic reproduction require that all industries which produce items of necessary consumption, whether for personal or productive use, must continue to operate and attract capital even if higher rates of profit can be gained elsewhere. A certain degree of mobility of capital from one industry to another can occur but there are definite limits beyond which this cannot proceed. For convenience we will assume that these limits have been reached and no mobility of capital is possible.

2. In our example the higher rate of profit in industry (2) is due to the fact that is has a lower organic composition of capital than industry (1). Having assumed equal rates of surplus value the variation in the rates of profit is due entirely to the organic composition of capital. Other things being equal, the higher the organic composition, the lower the rate of profit; which would indicate a tendency for capital to flow into industries where the organic composition of capital is below average. But as this runs counter to the tendency given by the process of accumulation for the organic composition of capital to rise, we must rule out large-scale mobility on these grounds.

We are therefore left with the problem that the conditions of production generate different average rates of profits between industries, but that economic conditions require these average rates of profit to be equal, and since this equality cannot be brought about by the movement of capital from one industry to another, only one possible method of equalising the rate of profit remains – variations in the price of commodities.

Let us recall the conditions of production in the two industries:

$$100c + 50v + 50s = 200o \qquad (1)$$
$$75c + 75v + 75s = 225o \qquad (2)$$

If both industries sell their outputs at prices equivalent to their values – i.e. if their prices are in the ratio 200:225 – then they gain different rates of profit: 33 per cent in industry (1) and 50 per cent in industry (2). This is the problem. But if industry (1) could put up its price above value and industry (2) reduced its price below value so that both sold their output at 212.5, they would each earn an equal rate of profit (41.66 per cent). The fact that this price is the same for both industries is accidental following the assumption that each industry advances the same amount of capital (150). What matters is the deviation of price from value whereby industry (1) sells for a price above value and industry (2) below value. There is no doubt that this procedure solves the problem in so far as it gives an equal rate of profit without any mobility of capital between industries, but it does so in a way that appears to create even more severe difficulties. A whole string of questions are immediately posed: 1. Is this really anything more than formal solution, just a simple arithmetic device? 2. Does not the deviation of prices from values undermine the theory of value? 3. What, if any, is the nature of the mechanism that brings about this solution, and what are its practical implications? To begin to answer these questions it is necessary to see in detail how the calculation is made.

The Transformation of Values into Prices of Production

		value $(c+v+s)$	cost price $(c+v)$	social rate of profit (p')	prices of production $(c+v) + p'(c+v)$
(1)	$100c + 50v + 50s$	200	150		212.5
(2)	$75c + 75v + 75s$	225	225		212.5
Social capital	$175c + 125v + 125s$	425	300	41.66%	425

In this schema we have entered the conditions of production of the two industries with which we are now familiar. We have then added these together to get the conditions of production for social capital, treating all the individual capitals in the economy as elements of a single whole. From this we calculate the social rate of profit, the rate of profit for social capital: $125s/175c + 125v = 41.66$ per cent. If each industry is to earn the same rate of profit, this is the rate it must be; so the next step is to calculate the *prices of production* at which each industry must sell its output to gain this rate of profit. (We must emphasise that these prices of production are not actual market prices expressed in money, but modified values that stipulate the ratio of money prices at which industries must sell to get an equal rate of profit — they are only the precursors of market prices.) This calculation is straightforward: we take the cost price for each industry – the amount of capital advanced – and add on to it the same amount deflated by the general rate of profit. Here, by chance, the cost price of production in both industries equals 150 and to this we add 41.66 per cent of 150 and get the total of 212.5. In the case of industry (1) it can be seen that the price of production is above value, with industry (2) it is below value. This explains the schema, but how does it answer our three questions?

1. *Is there any more than just a piece of arithmetic?* The answer depends upon the interpretation given to social capital. If it is just a simple total being no more than the sum of the individual capitals, then this is no more than a mathematical device that does not really solve the problem. If it is more than this, then the solution can make a substantial claim to validity. We will come back to this in a moment when considering the third question.

2. *Does the deviation of prices of production from values undermine the law of value?* This question has been the subject of fierce controversy which we cannot pretend to summarise adequately in the space available. For some critics the question can only be answered with an unambiguous yes, but their interpretation of the theory of value as a labour theory of prices, i.e. prices are proportionate to labour time, is undoubtedly wrong. As we pointed out in Chapters 2 and 3, equal exchange applies to all commodities taken together not to individual items, and it can be readily seen how this solution to the problem of the general rate of profit is consistent with that proposition. While it is possible, even necessary, that the price of production of a single commodity differs from its value, the prices of production of all commodities taken as a total equals the value of all commodities – both equal 425. Other critics have argued that this solution makes the value theory redundant and that it is possible to analyse the capitalist economy in terms of prices of production without any reference to value. To this we would respond that the prices of production are merely modified values, and that even if individual capitalists operate in terms of these prices and are unaware of value, nevertheless the capitalist economy is determined by the allocation and productivity of labour, both living and past. In other words, we would deny that the deviation of prices of

production from values undermines the law of value in any way at all, but add the cautionary note that a lot more can be said on the subject.

3. *What is the mechanism that brings this solution about and what are its practical implications?* This question takes us back to question 1, the nature of social capital, and obliges us to consider capitalism as a *social* system of production. Let us deal with social capital first. In the last section when considering competition, we saw that things are quite the reverse of how they look; it appears that individual capital is the basic unit of capitalist production, and that the development of the capitalist economy is the result of a mass of individual and independent initiatives. But in reality we saw that the freedom of the capitalist as capitalist is severely restricted; that if he does not satisfactorily pursue the requirements of accumulation he is driven out of business; and how competition is the medium through which these requirements were brought to bear upon him as an immanent necessity. Now we can state what is essentially the same point in different terms appropriate to the question under consideration here: it appears that social capital is merely the sum of individual capitals, but in reality the reverse is the case – individual capitals are merely the fragmented form of existence of social capital. Just as a wall, to take a very simple analogy, exists as a mass of bricks, so social capital exists as a mass of independent firms. But take a brick out of the wall and it ceases to be part of the wall; a firm outside social capital ceases to be a capitalist firm. What makes the analogy seem inappropriate are the different ways in which the elements cohere together: in the case of the wall, the individual bricks visibly support and complement each other; in the case of social capital, the individual capitals are at constant war with each other. This mutual antipathy of individual capitals is indeed a strange form of coherence, but that is the nature of the capitalist world and not an invention of theory. Like a couple held together by their psychological need to quarrel incessantly, individual capitals express their interdependence and their membership of the club, social capital, by continuous competition among themselves.

The other aspect of inter-capitalist dependence which expresses itself concretely at the level of use-value is easier to understand. A firm in one industry making, say, cars can only exist because other firms in other industries make the materials necessary for cars and produce the food and clothing necessary to sustain car workers. Here it is clear that capitalist production is a joint venture of capitalists because their activities visibly complement each other and need to dovetail if the system is to operate with any degree of coherence. We must now acknowledge that this coherence is not consciously planned but achieved unknowingly through the market where the capitalists confront each other as commodity owners and buy and sell as individual parties in competition, with each other. In other words, the unity of capital is evident at the level of use-value because the activities of independent firms visibly and necessarily complement each other: but this unity has to be effected through the exchange of commodities in terms of value, and here the means of effecting it appear as their opposite; as a fragmentation of capital into a vast army of independent elements. It is the cardinal feature of this solution that it combines both elements of this condition showing the unity of capital on the one hand, and the way in which this unity is achieved through competition, on the other. The point becomes clear as we trace its implications.

Suppose the higher organic composition of capital in industry (1) is indicative of a greater degree of concentration in that area of production. To make the situation clear cut, suppose industry (1) is dominated by a single monopoly while a large number of firms compete with each other in industry (2). Monopolistic power is the power to sell commodities at a price higher than that they would command under more competitive conditions: in the terms used here we can define it as the power to sell commodities not only above their value but also above their prices of production. The value of the output of industry (1) is 200, and the price of production that gives capital in this industry the general rate of profit is 212.5. Now suppose monopolisation allows this price of production to be pushed up to 250, everything else remaining the same. The rate of profit in industry (1) goes up to 66 per cent – i.e. price of production (250) less the cost price (150) as a percentage of the cost price – as the monopoly uses its power to gain a rate of profit higher than the general rate. But what the monopoly gains in one industry, the competitive firms must lose in the other, because the total pool of surplus value has not been increased. This pool is equal to 125, and if the monopoly in industry (1) is able to seize 100, only 25 remains for the competitive firms in industry (2). Since these firms have advanced a capital of 150, their average rate of profit falls to 16.6 per cent. A concentration of capital in industry (2) could redress the balance, but whatever the final result, one condition holds: as long as the conditions of production remain unchanged, monopolisation or any variation in the conditions of competition cannot affect the general rate of profit: hence it can only affect the distribution of profit between capitals. Although competition acts as an inducement to individual firms to alter the conditions of production in order to increase the rate of surplus value, directly it can do no more than alter the distribution of surplus value among different capitals.

We can now appreciate the ambiguity of inter-capitalist relations. On the one hand, individual capitals compete against each other to seize greater shares of the social pool of surplus value, and in this respect they are mortal enemies; on the other hand, they drink from the same cup and share a collective interest in defending it, and in increasing its contents as much as possible. Assume once again that firms in both industries earn the general rate of profit because of competition or countervailing monopolies, it does not matter. Now suppose that the firms (or firm) in industry (1) are able to double the rate of exploitation so that surplus value in industry (1) goes up from 50 to 100. Total surplus value increases from 125 to 175 and the general rate of profit rises correspondingly from 41.66 to 58.3 per cent: $175s/175c + 125v$. Firms in industry (2) benefit from this as much as those in industry (1), although they do nothing to bring it about. Equally, any reduction in the rate of exploitation in one industry reduces the rate of profit in the other, making it absolutely clear that although firms compete with each other, they nevertheless have strong mutual interests. In other words, although the organisation of social capital into a number of juridically independent firms sets one capital at the throat of another, as the appropriators of surplus value, as capital vis-à-vis labour, they form a regular masonic society. In class terms it amounts to this: competition, which divides capital into a series of warring factions, pales into insignificance against the common interest which all capitals share in opposition to the working class. The class force opposed to labour is *social capital*.

4. COMPETITION AND THE CLASS STRUGGLE

We must now consider the political aspects of competition, the role it plays in the relationship between capital and labour, and the problems posed by its decline in the political organisation of the class struggle. The central point here can be quickly stated: the fragmentation of social capital into a number of independent capitals simultaneously fragments the working class into a corresponding number of separate labour forces; but whereas these independent capitals can achieve a unity of purpose indirectly through the circulation of commodities, no such possibility is open to the working class. Whereas competition fragments labour completely, it fragments capital in a way that simultaneously unites it. In conditions of competition, capital is able to achieve its class purposes without any conscious organisation among individual capitalists; but the working class can only express its class interests through conscious organisation. This disparate effect of competition upon the classes is the key to unlocking a number of problems.

To begin, it is significant to note that for the main part opposition to monopolisation has been generated from within the capitalist camp and that, generally speaking, the working class has been antipathetic to political attempts to enforce conditions of 'fair' competition. There are sound economic reasons why this is the case: monopolisation, as we have just seen, has much more effect upon the distribution of surplus value among capitalists, than it does on the relation between capital and labour. In fact, monopolisation can work to the benefit of the working class in so far as it is associated with a rise in the organic composition of capital that increases productivity and permits increases in real wages. But the assiduity with which democratic states have pursued anti-monopolistic policies in the face of overwhelming odds cannot be satisfactorily explained in terms of political pressure from the representatives of small firms, or some nostalgic longing for a paradise lost; it is rooted in the constitution of the democratic state itself, and we must attempt to work out why this is the case if the problem of transforming values into prices of production is to be fully appreciated as something more than a technical footnote to the theory of value.

Since the second half of the nineteenth century, the capitalist class in the advanced countries has been forced to accept working class organisation and admit the presence of trade unionism as a feature of the economic landscape. But what it has tried very hard to avoid, sometimes by legislation, is the constitution of trade unions as *political* as opposed to *industrial* or *economic* organisations. In other words, it has been prepared to concede the right of workers to form unions to struggle at the level of the work-place against particular grievances and particular employers, but it has always frowned upon struggles that are more generally directed – sympathy strikes by one group of workers in support of others; and even worse, struggles aimed at securing concessions from the state. It is part of the democratic *credo* that industrial action should not be used to achieve political ends; that changes in the law, or other actions by the state, can only be initiated and authorised by a democratic assembly elected by individuals posited as citizens in whom all signs of class are extinguished. From this we can discern the theoretical and practical foundations of the democratic state: first, the separation of industrial action from political action, whereby the former features in the private domain as the business of individuals, or groups of individuals, and the latter is the monopoly of the state; and second, the neutrality of the state towards transactions in the private domain.

These two foundations are, of course, intimately related to each other; on the one side, the state can make no real claim to the monopoly of political power without effecting a separation of politics from economics; on the other side, this separation cannot be effected on democratic terms unless the state posits itself as neutral between different private or class interests. Thus it is perfectly consistent with the theory and practice of the democratic state to admit the existence of the class struggle, though the term is rarely used and more anodyne expressions like the 'two sides of industry' have replaced it. What is crucial is that the class struggle, by whatever name it is known, should be restricted to the private sphere and waged on a whole number of isolated fronts between particular capitals and the workers they employ. This definitive restriction of the class struggle in its open confrontations, its privatisation and localisation, does not mean for one moment that it is beyond the interest of the state, which has never stood passively by to let the contending parties get on with it as they will. On the contrary, the state has always been most deeply involved in its conduct; but to the extent that it acts as a democratic state, it must conduct its involvement with scrupulous impartiality between the contending parties. It is, of course, not by chance that it is through this very impartiality that the state acts systematically in the interests of one side; that through its neutrality it acts unfailingly in the interests of capital and against the interests of the working class, even where it takes issue against a particular capital.

It is in the very nature of things that no hard and fast distinctions can be made between what is industrial and economic on the one side, and what is political on the other. Nevertheless, we can usefully follow the conventional distinction which defines economic struggles as those centred on individual enterprises, or in some cases upon an industry, about wages and conditions of work; and political struggles as those which involve large sections of workers consciously organised as a class. Such a distinction underlies the theory and practice of the democratic state, and the point that is relevant for us is that it is a distinction more likely to be made effective in practice when capital is organised as large numbers of small competing firms. In such a situation, the unity of the working class, a unity that must be directly and consciously organised, is difficult to achieve; on the other hand, capital can achieve unity in these conditions indirectly through the market without any conscious effort or organisation on the part of the capitalists. In other words, as we noted at the start of this section, the competitive situation is biased in favour of capital, and any attempt by the state to enforce a rigorous separation of economics from politics must redound to its advantage. For a state-imposed separation of economics from politics is nothing more than a prohibition of directly organised links between different enterprises which the working class needs in order to act as a class, but which the capitalist class does not need, since it is able to achieve its class unity unconsciously through the market.

In this light, the connection between the democratic state and competitive capitalism can be clearly seen. But we must go further than talking of mere connections: the democratic state as we know it is a creature of competitive capitalism; it is the form of state most adequate to competitive capitalism. But having said this, we must recognise the decline of competition brought about by the process of accumulation, and accept the implication that the democratic state becomes progressively inadequate as the post-competitive phase of capitalism develops. Numerous reasons for this can be found among the critics of *laissez-faire* in the twentieth century, but only one interests us: the concentration of capital engendered by the process of accumulation has undermined the classical distinction between economic and political struggles upon which the theory and practice of the democratic state is based. Struggles can still take place in individual firms and can be safely ignored and contained within the general codes of the law; but many others have immediate and explosive implications which the state cannot so readily dismiss as economic, and lying beyond its sphere of direct interest. Thus, in the period since the end of the Second World War, we have seen a process developing, started during the War, of a complete restructuring of the institution of the state itself, the development of new bodies to intervene directly in the economic process. Moreover, the actions of these bodies cannot by the very nature of things be controlled by representative assemblies; and it is not by accident that many of the laws that most directly affect individuals come from the vast body of administrative law produced by these agencies, against which the elected assembly is an increasingly ineffective watchdog. In this way the liberal democratic ideals, in terms of which capitalism has asserted its superiority not only against the monstrous parody of communism practised in the Soviet Union but also against the as yet untried promise of communism, are in a process of decay brought about by the development of capitalism itself. The long post-war boom has disguised many of these developments and made them appear to be the acceptable price of prosperity. But the collapse of the boom and the need for the state to assume even greater responsibility for the management of accumulation is accelerating the process of democratic collapse which neither the nostalgic complaints of the conservatives, the clichéd reassurances of the social democrats, nor the high-minded appeals from even further to the left to maintain traditional freedoms, can alleviate.

5. HISTORICAL LIMITS

From variations in the organic composition of capital among the various firms and industries that comprise social capital, we turn to variations in the organic composition of social capital itself.

Consider the following schema where c, v and s have their usual meanings as constant and variable capital and surplus value; c' represents the organic composition of capital; s' the rate of surplus value; and p' the rate of profit.

$$
\begin{aligned}
&(1) \quad 20c + 80v + 80s - s' = 100\% \quad c' = \tfrac{1}{4} \quad p' = 80\% \\
&(2) \quad 40c + 60v + 60s - s' = 100\% \quad c' = \tfrac{2}{3} \quad p' = 60\% \\
&(3) \quad 60c + 40v + 40s - s' = 100\% \quad c' = 1\tfrac{1}{2} \quad p' = 40\% \\
&(4) \quad 80c + 20v + 20s - s' = 100\% \quad c' = 4 \quad p' = 20\%
\end{aligned}
$$

Here (1), (2), (3) and (4) represent social capital at successive periods and, for reasons outlined in the first section of this chapter, we assume that the organic composition of capital will rise. At the same time we suppose that the rate of surplus value remains constant with the result that the rate of profit declines steadily. Here, in its essence, is *the law of the falling tendency of the rate of profit* whose dramatic implications are obvious. The raison d'être of capital is accumulation and this, we know, is determined by the rate of profit. But as the process of accumulation increases the organic composition of capital rises and reduces the rate of profit; each advance in accumulation makes further progress more difficult until a point is reached where capital can no longer function. The law of the falling tendency of the rate of profit thus gathers all the contradictions of capitalism together into a succinct formula and for this reason it is not hard to understand why it has become the subject of fierce controversy. The most important question this controversy has raised concerns the long-term tendency of the rate of surplus value and it is on this issue that we shall concentrate.

The problem can be quickly summarised. This numerical schema does nothing more than state one of the formal properties of the rate of profit.

If we take the alternative way of expressing this rate, $\frac{s}{v} \div \left(1 + \frac{c}{v}\right)$, it is clear that since the organic composition of capital is in the denominator, any rise in it will reduce the rate of profit, *other things being equal*. Some doubts have been voiced about whether there is any systematic tendency for such a rise to occur, but of much greater importance for the integrity of the law as a law – i.e. as a necessary tendency of capitalist development – are the suppositions hidden in the qualification 'other things being equal'. The most important 'other thing' here is the rate of surplus value, and it is clear that an increase causes the rate of profit to go up, just as surely as an increase in the organic composition of capital causes it to fall. Thus, if we assume the rate of surplus value rises to 133 per cent in period (2) of our schema; 200 per cent in period (3); and 400 per cent in period (4), the rate of profit remains constant at the period (1) level of 100 per cent, despite the increase in the organic composition of capital. Furthermore, any growth of the rate of surplus value by amounts greater than these causes the rate of profit to rise. To this formal point the critics of the law add a substantial one. The reason for the rise in the organic composition of capital, they point out, is alterations in the process of production precisely in order to increase the rate of surplus value; what happens to the rate of profit depends upon the extent to which they are successful. They conclude that there are no systematic forces working in one direction or the other; that the long-term movement of the rate of profit cannot be expressed in a legal fashion, since it is determined by a balance of probabilities with no grounds for predicting whether the balance will tilt in one direction or another.

Any reasonable defence of the law must concede the main points of this criticism right away. Firstly, the assumption of a constant rate of surplus value is only a convenience to illustrate the effects of rises in the organic composition of capital. Secondly, the probability of increases in the organic composition causing the rate of surplus to rise sufficiently to maintain the rate of profit or even to permit it to rise, must also be admitted. Thirdly, a whole series of other 'counter-acting factors' must be recognised: the possibility of wages being held down below value; a fall in the relative value of the means of production; the expansion of capital into new areas; an increase in the rate of turnover and so on. In other words, only when we reject the law as an empirical generalisation, i.e. as a prediction of how the rate of profit will actually move, can we begin to understand what its real meaning is and put up a rational defence of its tenets.

In the final analysis, the criticism of the law of the falling rate of profit is formal, and in this sense abstract. The substantive point that increases in the organic composition of capital can induce compensating rises in the rate of surplus value has never really been at issue. But the other point that it is always possible to posit a rate of surplus value, no matter how high, to maintain the rate of profit, treats the question as though it were simply a matter of numbers. Consider the extreme situation where the organic composition of capital rises to the point at which variable capital equals zero. Here capitalist production simply ceases to exist, since zero variable capital means no living labour is employed in the process of production, hence no value is produced, no surplus value and no profit. We can call this situation the *absolute limit* of capitalist production, and if we make this the point of departure for analysis things appear to be very different. We must make it clear that this limit should not be conceived in rigid terms, implying that capitalism can continue to function up to the point when variable capital finally disappears. Like the gravitational field of a heavenly body which operates deep into space, the influence of this limit makes itself felt far beyond its strict definition. As variable capital falls, first relative to constant capital and then absolutely, the number of workers employed decreases. At the absolute limit there are no workers, but capital could scarcely operate with a mere handful who supervised automatic equipment, since the rate of surplus value necessary to make any venture profitable in such a situation lies beyond the realms of plausibility. This is the crux of the matter. The reduction of variable capital to zero, totally automated and self-regulating production, may not be a technical possibility, but production that requires very few workers certainly is. In other words, there are no insuperable barriers to the extent to which production can be mechanised and every advance in technology has pushed the practical limits outwards rather than exhausted the possibilities of further progress. On the other hand, the rates of surplus value needed to maintain the rate of profit at very high levels of the organic composition of capital are simply not plausible. It is one thing to enter numbers in a schema, it is quite another to manage a society in which the great mass of the people have no economic function and a small group of workers are exploited at astronomic rates.

The law of the tendency of the falling rate of profit thus finally reduces itself to the tendency of the organic composition of capital to rise; and the criticism that this can be compensated by induced rises in the rate of surplus value carries no weight when capitalism has advanced to very high stages. But this still leaves a crucial question unanswered: how far must capitalism develop before the rate of surplus value peaks and the rate of profit begins to fall? Has this stage been reached already, or does it belong to some indefinite future that always recedes over the horizon? Take the concept of the absolute limit of capitalist production. It is crucial to understand that this is not a prediction of the future, a forecast of things to come, but a theoretical summary of the possibilities already given by the nature of capitalism and its development. In this sense it is an immanent feature of capitalist production, present all the time, just as the certainty of death is present all the time in the life of every living creature; just as death is a condition of life shaping every moment, even when it is consciously believed remote, so the development of capitalism is suffused with the immanent possibility of its demise.

There is always the danger of confusing logical sequence with temporal sequence, for it is convenient to think in terms of time as though one thing that follows another logically comes after it later. This often colours the way we think about structures where it is easy to slip from an analysis of anatomy into a logical projection about its development and talk as though the future was already determined as a logically necessary outcome of the present. The law of the falling tendency of the rate of profit is easily misunderstood in this way and seen as a process that must inevitably start sometime or other, whereas in fact it has always existed, even when the rate of profit has been rising. Or to put it another way that is less confusing, the absolute limits of capitalist development which this law allows us to perceive and express convenient are not a point in the future but a permanent condition of its existence. This, in fact, says nothing more than that capitalism has *historical limits*, that it is a historical form of social organisation in the sense that it has not always existed and there are many things that cannot be achieved within its framework.

These things, it cannot be stressed too strongly, are not mere trifles to be dismissed as irrelevant. On the contrary they are possibilities created by capitalism itself which it strives to achieve but at its peril, like the mechanisation of production; or expectations that it has aroused and made feasible, but which it can never concede, like equality and economic security and prosperity.

8 The Return of the Reserve Army

After the Second World War and the period of recovery, there followed a twenty-year phase of expansion unparalleled in capitalist history. As the boom established itself in the fifties, the claim that the old problems of capitalism had at last been superseded gained ground steadily; though today, as the world economy settles into its deepest recession since the thirties, it is clear that their disappearance was only temporary. But for more than twenty-five years after the War nobody seriously challenged the view that Keynes' *General Theory*, published in 1936, had unravelled the intricacies of the capitalist economy in a way that provided governments with a blueprint for successful economic management. The maintenance of full employment and sustained economic growth only confirmed the Keynesian view of political economy, that the capitalist economy can be controlled by a combination of monetary and fiscal policies, and the interpretation of modern history that gives Keynesianism the credit for the boom. In the face of this triumph, revolutionary criticism was reduced to radical opposition, as it accepted the main tenets of Keynesianism and explained how capitalism had changed, and how the class struggle between labour and capital had been replaced by a conflict between the developed and underdeveloped countries that cut across the old class boundaries. Now, after five years of recession with few signs of full recovery in sight, the Keynesian final solution seems less permanent than it did a decade ago, and ideas that were almost unthinkable during the hey-day of the boom now demand serious attention. As the total of the jobless mounts in the advanced countries and analyses indicate that full employment requires rates of economic growth that appear impossible to achieve, the relationship between accumulation and unemployment has once again become an open question. Throughout the boom the advanced countries used immigration and the movement of guest workers to turn the underdeveloped world into a reservoir of available workers; but now the *reserve army of labour* is permanently camped within the heartlands of capitalism as a threat to social peace.

1. ACCUMULATION AND UNEMPLOYMENT

At any moment the amount of employment in a capitalist economy is determined by the size of variable capital and the average value of labour-power. Thus:

$$e = \frac{v}{l}$$

where e represents the level of employment; v the size of variable capital; and l the average value of labour-power. Thus if l equals £60 per week (£3,000 per annum) and v equals £6 million, there is a level of employment, e, of 2,000 jobs. If the value of labour-power remains constant but variable capital falls to £4.5 million, employment falls to 1,500 jobs. But should the value of labour-power fall at the same time to £45 per week (£2,250 a year) employment will remain the same. To discover how employment varies with the accumulation of capital, it follows that we must discover how accumulation affects the size of variable capital on the one side, and the value of labour-power on the other. This can be done theoretically in four stages.

1. *All surplus value is consumed personally by the capitalists; the value of labour-power remains constant; but the organic composition of capital rises.* Under these conditions employment varies directly with variable capital, which in turn changes with the organic composition of capital; i.e. there is a direct connection between the level of employment and the organic composition of capital with the one falling as the other rises.

If we let K represent total capital advanced $(c + v)$; and k, the organic composition of capital (c/v) we get the following:

$$v = \frac{K}{1 + k}$$

If $v = £6$ million and c is the same, then $K = £12$ million and $k = 1$. Now suppose that k rises to 1.66, but K remains constant at £12 million (i.e. zero accumulation); v falls to £4.5 million, and assuming the value of labour-power is unchanged, the level of employment falls. This restates the proposition contained in the formula $e = v/l$, but it does so in a way that takes account of the organic composition of capital, and thereby allows us to draw a conclusion about the relationship between employment and accumulation: *as the accumulation of capital leads to a rise in its organic composition, the level of employment falls other things being equal.*

2. *The rate of accumulation is positive, but the organic composition of*

capital and the value of labour-power remain constant. From the formula $v = \frac{K}{1+k}$, it is clear that in so far as accumulation increases total capital advanced, K, but leaves the organic composition, k, unchanged, the size of variable capital rises; and if the value of labour-power remains constant employment also goes up. Thus we have a second conclusion: *other things being equal employment rises with the accumulation of capital.*

3. *The value of labour-power remains constant; the rate of accumulation is positive and the organic composition of capital rises.* This is a critical case that combines (1) and (2) where the movement of employment depends upon the differential of the rate of accumulation on the one hand, and the organic composition of capital, on the other. At first sight it would appear that strict proportionality holds, so that a rate of accumulation of, say 50 per cent, would balance a tendency of the organic composition of capital to grow at the same rate. But as the following schema shows this is not the case:

Variable capital £m (1)	Organic composition of capital (2)	Total capital advanced £m (3)	Growth in the rate of accumulation per cent (4)
6.0	1.00	12.0	–
6.0	1.66	16.0	1.33
6.0	2.76	22.6	1.41
6.0	4.58	33.6	1.49

Column (3) shows how much capital has to be advanced to maintain the level of variable capital (1) when the organic composition of capital grows at a steady rate. This rate (not shown in the table) is 166 per cent: against it we must set the growth in the rate of accumulation, column (4); and it is clear that (i) the two rates are not equal, and (ii) the rate of accumulation grows as the organic composition of capital reaches higher levels. Thus to our conclusions so far we can add this additional point: *an increase in the organic composition of capital tends to reduce the level of employment*; or to be more precise, *as the organic composition of capital rises the rate of accumulation must grow even faster if the level of variable capital is to be maintained.* But as we saw in the last chapter a growth in the organic composition of capital tends to restrict accumulation by depressing the rate of profit; so that the development which makes higher rates of accumulation necessary tends, at the same time, to make them more difficult. As we will see more clearly in a moment the forces that determine the level of employment are the same as those that produce the falling tendency of the rate of profit.

4. *The value of labour-power changes; the rate of accumulation is positive and the organic composition of capital grows.* A fall in the value of labour-power increases employment and this can compensate inadequacies in the rate of accumulation depending, of course, on the magnitudes involved. But such a fall requires an increase in productivity in the wage-goods sector, and this, in turn, depends upon an increase in the organic composition of capital. So here we have a conclusion that runs counter to the one above: *an increase in the organic composition of capital, in so far as it increases productivity and reduces the value of wage-goods, cuts the value of labour-power and increases the level of employment.* Thus movements in the level of employment like movements in the rate of profit depend upon the balance between the two opposite consequences of increases in the organic composition of capital. The connection between profitability and employment is therefore very close.

We have seen that the level of employment depends upon the size of variable capital and the value of labour-power.

Thus: $$e = \frac{v}{l}$$

But: $$v = \frac{K}{1+k}$$

Hence: $$e = \frac{K}{1+k} \cdot \frac{1}{l} \qquad (1)$$

At the same time the rate of profit (p'):

$$p' = \frac{s}{v} \div \left(1 + \frac{c}{v}\right)$$

substituting k for the organic composition of capital:

$$= \frac{s}{v} \div (1+k) \qquad (2)$$

The similarities between equation (1), the level of employment, and equation (2), the rate of profit, are immediately striking. To begin with both have the same denominator, $(l+k)$, showing that both tend to fall as the organic composition of capital rises. At the same time, this fall can be compensated in both cases by the effects that a rise in the organic composition of capital has upon their respective numerators; which, in their turn, are variants of each other. The reciprocal of the value of labour-power (1/l) is a perfect correlate of the rate of surplus value; while the level of capital advanced equals the absolute amount of surplus value. There are circumstances in which the two ratios can move in opposite directions with the rate of profit going up and the level of employment coming down; but as these do not affect our conclusions here we will leave them aside and consider only the general case where employment and profitability move together. As the reason for employing labour in capitalist society is the production of surplus value and its appropriation as profit, we should not be surprised that the rate of profit and the level of employment are so intimately connected and correlate so closely. But if we accept this conclusion we must also accept its implications: since the structure of capitalist production imparts an immanent tendency for the rate of profit to fall, so it must also impart a similar tendency on the level of employment: on the one side, a falling tendency of the rate of profit; on the other, a progressive decline in the level of employment. In other words, the analysis that leads to the law of the falling tendency of the rate of profit brings us to *the progressive production of a reserve army of industrial labour* as an immanent characteristic of capitalist development.

2. THE 'DOUBLE-CRISIS'

This analysis, with its conclusion of unavoidable unemployment, stands in sharp opposition to the confidence, initiated by Keynesian theory and consolidated in the boom, that, so long as it is properly managed, the capitalist economy can be stabilised at full employment. Contained in this opposition are issues of crucial significance for the present situation which need the most careful definition. The difficulties are even greater than they first appear, and we must start by clearing away the most important source of confusion by recognising that Keynesianism, both in theory and in practice, addresses itself to a different aspect of the problem of unemployment from that with which the theory of the progressive production of the reserve industrial army deals.

First Keynesianism, despite its protestations of internationalism, makes the national economy its focus of attention and, moreover, the national economy of the advanced capitalist country. This follows from its preoccupation with policy and its inevitable acceptance of the (national) state as the agent of policy. Its concern with the so-called underdeveloped world has never been more than nominal; while its attention to international economic relations has in the main restricted itself to financial relations among developed countries. Thus the relationship between the developed and underdeveloped worlds has been peripheral to its main concerns; but as large-scale migration between the two shows, this relationship plays a critical role in determining conditions in the labour market. The achievement of full employment in the post-war period reveals itself as incomplete once we drop this nationalist perspective, and recognise that the masses of the underdeveloped world, living outside the immediate confines of industrial capitalism, form a vast reservoir of spare labour. Admittedly a distinction exists between this reservoir, due to the peculiarly incomplete development of capitalism on a world scale (i.e. underdevelopment), and unemployment arising from within industrial capitalism as the composition of accumulation creates a declining number of jobs; but it is not as great as the nationalist Keynesian would like to believe. We can only note this point as a qualification to our own analysis, which the pressure of space forces us to restrict to the potential of unemployment within the framework of industrial capitalism narrowly defined. But it is important to realise the assumptions embodied in such a restriction. From its beginnings in the eighteenth century, industrial capitalism has consistently maintained a reservoir of spare labour on its peripheries, and ignoring it on the grounds that it has a coloured skin or talks a foreign language, is nationalistic hypocrisy.

Second, Keynesianism has always adopted a short-term approach to the problem of unemployment and considered economic processes in a time dimension where the forces that produce the reserve army do not operate. Thus Keynes himself restricted his attention to causes of instability that excluded variations in the organic composition of capital which alter the structural demand for labour in the economy; and his followers have kept more or less within these guidelines. The most cogent explanation of this restriction is that it isolates economic variables which are amenable to state policy and ignores others, like the rate and composition of accumulation, which the state cannot control without undermining the very foundations of capitalist production. To the extent that unemployment can be created by forces operating within the interstices of the accumulation process and that these can be subjected to a degree of state control, Keynesian political economy stands on solid ground. The most important short-term cause of unemployment and general instability in the capitalist economy is the discrepancy between the two aspects of the wage-form we analysed in Chapter 6; and although it is not conceived in these terms, this discrepancy occupies a central position in the Keynesian system. It will be recalled that the wage-form comprises the value of labour-power on the one side, which determines the rates of surplus value and profit appropriate for the prevailing conditions of production; and the value of labour, on the other. The latter is the form in which the wage exists and it is in terms of the value of labour that wages are negotiated between the classes. This qualitative differentiation of the two aspects of the wage-form creates the *formal possibility* (i.e. a possibility given by the wage-form itself) of quantitative discrepancy whereby the value of labour, wages as they are actually paid, differs from the value of labour-power. If the former exceed the latter, the rates of surplus value and profit are driven below their appropriate level and the conditions for depression exist. Part of the Keynesian analysis (the multiplier process) is concerned with how such a discrepancy in one sector of the economy can generalise itself to others, and create a cyclical downturn in economic activity out of proportion to the original imbalance; while the practical aspects of Keynesianism propose methods to prevent such an imbalance occurring in the first place, or to contain its effects if it does occur. The greater stability of the post-war period relative to earlier times, indicates how effective Keynesianism has been; but can this success continue? Recent capitalist developments are calling short-term stabilising measures into question and a growing number of critics believe they make matters worse, rather than better.

A clear theoretical distinction can be made in terms of the rate and composition of accumulation between conditions where stabilisation policies can be effective and others where their efficiency must be in doubt. Thus if the rate of accumulation and the composition of capital are such as to provide jobs for the whole of the available labour-force, there is little doubt that a stabilisation policy can dampen down short-term fluctuations that threaten full employment. But if the conditions of accumulation fall short of the full employment level, new problems present themselves. Suppose for the sake of argument that the rate of accumulation, the value of labour-power and the organic composition of capital are of a size that creates jobs for only 90 per cent of the workforce, leaving a structural employment gap of 10 per cent: what can short-term stabilisation policies achieve here? Clearly they can stabilise the *unemployment* equilibrium and dampen down fluctuations around it; but can they bring the economy up to full employment? The answer to this question falls into two parts. In so far as short term monetary and fiscal measures cannot directly alter the rate and composition of accumulation and can affect it indirectly only to a limited extent, the answer must be

The Return of the Reserve Army

no – short term measures cannot plug a structural employment gap. On the other hand, a systematic extension of fiscal policy where a government runs a deficit to finance expenditure on health and welfare programmes, public works and defence, underwrites the losses of nationalised industries and subsidises unprofitable private firms, can create 'new' jobs; and if the deficit is large enough it can bring the economy to full employment. So the question can be answered positively as well as negatively and once again we are faced with the type of equivocal conclusion that we have met so many times before.

In analysing the movement of wages in Chapter 6, we saw how the impossibility of reaching any definite conclusion as to whether wages rise or fall with capitalist development arises from the complex nature of the wage-form, which allows an increase in one aspect of the wage to be accompanied by a fall in another. The same complexity surrounds employment; and the same possibilities of ambiguity. At first sight the question of employment seems simple and straightforward: employment means jobs; full employment is where everyone has a job and unemployment where there are not enough jobs to go round. This is the *employment of labour*; but just as important in the capitalist economy is the *employment of capital* – whether it is idle or actively engaged in the acquisition of surplus value. In other words there are two aspects to the question of full employment – the full employment of labour and the full employment of capital – and there is no reason why the qualitative difference between them cannot express itself quantitatively. Just as a discrepancy can arise between the two aspects of the wage and the value of labour can exceed the value of labour-power, so a discrepancy can arise between the two aspects of employment. In fact it is exceptional for the two to coincide, since there is no mechanism in the capitalist economy to bring them into line with each other. If the two happen to coincide, as appears to have been the case in the post-war period, it is more the result of chance than deliberate state policy; and in this light we interpret the success of Keynes-inspired stabilisation policies in achieving full employment as the result of a happy coincidence of circumstances that no longer applies.

So far we have distinguished the formal causes of unemployment that preoccupied Keynes from the structural causes associated with the rate and composition of accumulation in traditional economic terms of the short period and the long period. But cutting across this distinction and revealing the political charge hidden in the 'scientific' neutrality of its language, is the antipathy between the two aspects of employment couched in explicit class terms. Thus Keynesianism is concerned not only with employment in the short period, but with employment from the point of view of capital; and in the last analysis its concept of full employment is the full employment of capital; though as we might expect, even this is mystified both theoretically and politically. The theoretical grounds for confusion lie in the fact that the employment of capital is invariably posited in terms of labour: thus, although reference is made to under-utilised capacity and idle money, it is more normal to talk of unemployed steelworkers, shipyard workers or whatever, when what is really meant is unemployed capital in the steel industry, the shipbuilding industry and so on. The political grounds of confusion find their ultimate origins in the deep-seated reluctance of the various representatives of the capitalist order to acknowledge the fundamental opposition of class interests which the distinction between the employment of labour and the employment of capital makes explicit. The importance of this misrepresentation of Keynesianism as a political economy centred on the full employment of labour cannot be exaggerated. Not only did it allow the state to renew its claim to represent the interests of every section of society in terms relevant to the new conditions of capitalism which emerged through the depression of the thirties, but it also provided a coherent political and ideological framework for trade union participation in the capitalist project which defined the job-security of the working class as the main criterion of its success. So long as the full employment of labour and capital coincided through the fifties and sixties, even though by chance rather than design, the distinction between them remained abstract and unimportant, and solid grounds existed for class coalition and concensus politics.

But what happens when the two aspects of full employment no longer coincide? We considered this situation above and saw that it was possible for the state to plug the (labour) employment gap by deficit financing expenditures on public works etc. – a strategy which in many people's minds has come to represent the hallmark of Keynesianism. When the trade union movement calls for an end to cuts in public expenditure and an expansionary economic policy, it is exactly this type of policy it has in mind. But underlying this attempt to appropriate Keynesianism for the working class are a number of highly dubious assumptions. Firstly, that Keynesianism comprises objective analyses and policies which have no particular class moorings. This, of course, runs counter to Keynes' own conception – he was explicit in affirming his personal solidarity with the bourgeoisie and his political allegiance to the capitalist order even though he wanted the one to be educated and the other to be reformed. But, secondly, and for our purpose more importantly, this call for deficit financed expansion usually presupposes that only a temporary boost is needed, and that once pushed in an upward direction the system can defy the laws of economic gravity and maintain the full employment of labour by itself. In other words, it presupposes that a policy of financial expansion can alter the structural conditions of production and bring about an upward shift in the level of (capital) full employment. But there is no evidence either theoretical or empirical to support this view. On the contrary, all the evidence suggests that if the employment gap is anything but very small or temporary, persistent deficit finance creates more problems than it solves.

The consequences of sustained deficit expenditure vary according to a whole series of conditions too detailed for us to consider here – e.g. the scale and duration of the deficit and the methods used to finance it; the type of activities sponsored and the international position of the country, its balance of payments, reserve position and so on. But outside the ranks of the radical Keynesians, there now seems to be general agreement that attempts to maintain full employment by prolonged deficit expenditure generate chronic inflation, although an acrimonious controversy rages as to exactly how this comes about. From our perspective the processes at work here can be summarised along the following lines:

1. Workers employed with money made available by the state exclusively for the purpose of creating jobs do not produce surplus value. This proposition is virtually a definition: if unemployed workers were a potential source of surplus value their labour-power would be purchased directly by capital and state intervention would not be necessary.

2. But in many cases, it happens that workers employed with state money do not even produce value. This is not a definition, since many state employed workers, those in the nationalised industries for example, do produce value and even surplus value. Nevertheless there are other areas of state employment in the social services, health, education, certain types of public work and administration, police and defence, where the results of labour are not commodities that are realised for money. It is true that this type of labour is essential for capitalist society, and must be financed by the state even when there are no problems of chronic unemployment; also it is possible for this labour to make a positive contribution to value production elsewhere in the economy, though generally speaking it only does so after a fairly long lapse of time. But we are only interested in the 'excessive' employment of this labour which has taken place in various capitalist countries in the last fifteen or so years.

3. Labour that does not produce value does not produce the value

equivalent of its wage, but at the end of the week, the workers enter the market with money which is indistinguishable from the money advanced as variable capital to those who have produced a value equivalent. In other words, money is injected via the wages of state paid workers into the system of circulation without any corresponding commodity-value from the sphere of production.

4. At the best of times the complex formal structure of the production and realisation of value makes for a highly unstable situation, since the only mechanism spontaneously created by the capitalist economy to balance the mass of value produced on the one side, with the conditions of circulation (money) on the other, is cyclical fluctuation – i.e. short-term 'Keynesian crisis'. Any employment policy that relies heavily on deficit financing only adds to this instability, and, to this extent, it increases the dangers of a 'short-term' crisis on top of the chronic problems that already exist. There are signs that this type of *double crisis* is already in motion, causing a leading financial journal to forecast that 'things are likely to get worse before they get even worse'.

The crux of the matter is that the inequality of the full employment of capital and the full employment of labour is created in the sphere of production, by the conditions of accumulation on the one hand, and the size of the available labour force on the other. The application of Keynesian measures does not resolve it; rather it displaces it into the sphere of circulation where it persists in a new form as an imbalance between money and commodity-values. In other words, the treatment of chronic long-term unemployment with monetary and fiscal measures changes its mode of expression, and gives it a new form of appearance and existence as a monetary and fiscal problem that is apparently amenable to orthodox Keynesian remedies. Thus governments throughout the western world and, particularly in the weaker capitalist countries—the UK, Italy, France, Spain, Canada and to some extent the United States—diagnose the difficulties that beset their economies in traditional terms and respond with more or less traditional measures. The hypothesis we advance here about the nature of the present crisis – hypothesis only because the analysis to substantiate it is absent – stands in total opposition to the official view. It has three parts. First, the disjuncture that has ended the long post-war boom has originated in the sphere of production through developments in the rate and composition of accumulation. Second, the fact that it has assumed the symptomatic forms of a temporary recession, such as monetary and fiscal imbalance, is due to attempts by various states to find jobs for every worker after the full employment of capital had fallen below the full employment of labour – a process which in all probability began in the mid-sixties. We might add that the migration of manufacturing capital to parts of the underdeveloped world that began around the same time has exacerbated the situation, but probably not to the extent where it could be completely alleviated by import controls. *Third*, by displacing the disequilibrium into the sphere of circulation, official measures have added to the endemic short-term instability of the capitalist economy and established conditions for a *double crisis*, already expressing itself in the completely novel juxtaposition of inflation and unemployment.

Note: Productive and Unproductive Labour

In Chapter 1 we defined the irrationality of capitalist production in its most general terms, as an opposition between the production of wealth on the one side, and the absolute poverty of the working class, on the other. As productivity improves, this irrationality asserts itself as a series of contradictions within capitalism between what are often called the forces and the relations of production. This perspective is inadequate rather than false, and we are now in a position to see its limitations. If the analysis is not developed beyond this stage, the irrationality of capitalism can appear as though it were only partial; since it is consistent with this view to define capitalism as essentially a mode of producing use-values to satisfy human needs, but one which is distorted and made inefficient by its particular social organisation (production for need versus production for profit). This perspective is encapsulated in the definition of productive labour in terms of use-value. In fact, the irrationality of capitalist production is complete and the production of use-values is nothing more than an inevitable but incidental constraint upon accumulation. Hence the practical definition of productive labour in capitalist society is not that labour which produces use-values, but that which produces surplus value. The usefulness of a product does not count here; or even the fact that it is necessary and indispensible for social reproduction: the preoccupation of capital with its own self-expansion is so complete that everything else is incidental. Only that labour which produces surplus value is productive, the rest is unproductive.

Two sets of objections have been levelled against this definition: one denies any distinction between productive and unproductive labour; the other accepts it, but claims that the criterion of surplus value alone is too restrictive. For the last hundred years the first position has been a canon of economic orthodoxy, the argument being that labour which produces something useful is productive; and since the criterion of usefulness is whether or not its direct or indirect embodiment can be sold, it follows that all paid labour must be productive. Those who subscribe to the second set of objections reproduce this argument in favour of use-value as a criterion for defining productive labour, though admittedly in less crude ways: hence we can concentrate upon them exclusively, since any criticism here applies *a fortiori*. Although quite different lines of attack are developed, a common theme runs throughout them all: always the argument comes back to the point that the criteria by which labour is judged, productive or unproductive, must include the nature and usefulness of the product; and it is on these grounds that we reject them all.

For convenience we can summarise these objections under three heads:

Note: Productive and Unproductive Labour

1. Many types of labour that do not produce surplus value directly, nonetheless make an indispensable contribution to it—work in health, education, scientific research, etc. and, most contentious of all, domestic work. These and similar types of labour can only be realistically classified as productive.

2. Only labour that contributes directly or indirectly to the process of social reproduction is productive; the remainder which produces luxury goods, armaments etc. is unproductive. Here the criticism is that the definition of productive labour in terms of surplus value takes no account of the imperatives of social life.

3. The rigid application of surplus value as the criterion by which to judge labour productive or unproductive, leads inevitably to inconsistencies, since the same type of labour is productive in one place and unproductive in the next. For example, when a nurse works for a private profit-making clinic she is a productive worker, but when she works for a state-financed hospital, that gives its services free, she is unproductive.

Each of these points can be elaborated in detail, but even a summary as brief as this shows that the objection is always the same: the definition of productive labour must include the material nature of the product. Any definition which refuses this must be unrealistic and irrational for reasons which each line of criticism makes obvious in its different way: it refuses to acknowledge the undeniable contribution of many workers who do not produce surplus value directly; it ignores altogether the question of social reproduction; and, finally, it leads to all manner of inconsistencies. But paradoxically this is precisely the point we wish to make. The definition of productive labour as only that labour which produces surplus value is not a theoretical definition made for the purposes of studying capitalism, but a practical definition made by capitalism in its *modus operandi*. Hence valid objections to it on the grounds that it is unrealistic, irrational or inconsistent are properly directed against capitalism itself.

We have seen that in capitalist society all production is subject to the control of capital and contained within the circuit, $M \ldots P \ldots M'$. The ideal form of this circuit, which states its only possible *raison d'être*, is $M - M'$, where production is dispensed with altogether. Since this is impossible, capital is forced to accept the inevitability of material production, but only on condition that it becomes a process for producing surplus value. The definition of productive labour as only that labour which produces surplus value directly, merely restates this point: that is to say, it expresses the ideal principle of capital according to which it organises the world. Confusion arises, again in practice first, then in theory, over a subsequent question: how far can capital succeed with this project? How far can it succeed in deposing labour as a primary activity through which men appropriate their needs from nature, and in transforming it into a value producing process that creates surplus value?

The extent to which labour can be perverted depends upon its productivity and the development of material production. Consider two situations: one where 90 per cent of production is necessary and only 10 per cent is surplus; and another where 10 per cent is necessary and 90 per cent is surplus. In the first, the freedom of capital, the autonomy of value vis-à-vis use-value, is severely restricted in comparison with the second, where the physical requirements of reproduction offer many fewer constraints on the production of value and the unimpeded pursuit of surplus value. Hence the paradox that capital develops material production to the highest possible levels through disinterest. At the same time, it can never develop it to the point where it ceases to exercise some influence, however residual, upon the structure and composition of production. But this residual influence which diminishes with every advance in the development of the social forces of production, provides only the most paltry grounds for insisting that the criterion of usefulness plays a significant role in determining what is and what is not productive labour, or, more generally, that the satisfaction of human needs is anything but an incidental side-effect of capitalist production.

Suggested Reading

Ultimately there is no substitute for reading Karl Marx himself, but before tackling *Capital*, which is best read in a study group, it often helps to read simpler works, such as the *Communist Manifesto* and *Value, Price and Profit*. *Capital* itself is most easily approached by reading Parts 3 and 4 before the more inaccessible earlier sections.

The best of the many introductory books are:
Paul M. Sweezy, *The Theory of Capitalist Development*, Modern Reader Paperbacks, New York and London.
Earnest Mandel, *Marxist Economic Theory*, Merlin Press, London.
William J. Blake, *Elements of Marxian Economic Theory and its Criticism*, Cordon Company, New York.
(This is far the best of the introductory books, but it is long out of print.)

The more advanced books are:
I. I. Rubin, *Essays on Marx's Theory of Value*, Black and Red, Detroit.
Roman Rosdolsky, *The Making of Marx's 'Capital'*, Pluto Press, London.

Other works of economic interest include:
P. Baran, and P. N. Sweezy, *Monopoly Capitalism*, Penguin Books, London.
Harry Braverman, *Labour and Monopoly Capital*, Modern Reader Paperbacks, London and New York.

Short works of philosophical interest include:
Karl Korsch, *Marxism and Philosophy*, New Left Books, London.
Karl Marx, *Early Writings,* Penguin Books, London (see the introduction by Lucio Colletti).

Index

Abstract labour, 15, 23–4, 26, 31, 60
Accumulation, 28, 29, 101
   capitalist, 30, 54, 62, 77, 100, 116
   speed of, 79, 81, 83, 92–3
   strategies, 47
   and unemployment, 121–4
Adequation of material to value production, 54–5
Agriculture, production in, 94

Banking capital, 101–2
Barter, direct, 12, 17, 20, 27; *see also* Exchange

Capital
   advanced, 80
   banking, 101–2
   circuit of, 29–30, 31, 32, 40, 42
   circulation, and wages, 86–8
   concentration of, 97–104
   constant, 42–3, 67, 93
   definition of, 29–30
   employment of, 80, 127, 128, 130
   industrial, circuit of, 32–4
   interdependence, social, 50, 104
   organic composition of, 93–7, 99, 106, 111, 118, 121–4
   as production factor, 8–9
   social, 31, 39, 49, 104–12
      organic composition, variations in, 116–19
   technical composition of, 94, 95–7
   turnover, time needed, 78–85, 93
   value composition of, 94–5
   variable, 42, 44, 50, 93
   and employment, 121
Capitalism
   accumulation, 30, 54, 62, 77, 100, 116
   and class division, 30, 76–7, 89–91, 112–16, 120

competition, 50, 98–101, 110, 111–12, 112–16
   and control, 55, 57, 58, 67, 89–91
   inter-capitalist transactions, 39, 40, 104–12
   irrationality of, ix, 6, 54, 77–8, 132
   Keynesian theory, 120
   and machinery, 63–7
   managers in, 101–4
   ownership of firms, 101–3
   production, 25, 57–8, 60–1, 62
   social relations of, 50, 96, 104, 110–11
   and the state, 115–16
   and surplus value, maximum, 40–1, 55
   wealth, inequality of, 1, 44, 58
   work, necessity of, 4, 35–6, 96
   and working class consumption, 87, 100
Circuit of basic reproduction, 10
Circuit of capital, general form, 29–30, 31, 32, 40, 42
Circuit of industrial capital, 32–4
Circuit of labour, 30
Circuit of simple circulation, 27–30
Circulation
   capitalist, 86–8
   simple, 27–30
Class struggle, 30, 76–7, 89–91, 112–16, 120
Coins, 18
Commodities, 11
   exchange value, 20–1, 26
   labour, products of, 14–15, 21–3, 26
   money, relations between, 13–17, 26
   necessary for labour-power, 9–10, 36, 37–8, 46, 48, 50, 85–6, 94, 101

Index

production, simple, 25
use value, 20, 22, 26
value, 21–2
Communism, 9, 104, 115
Competition, 50, 98–101, 110, 111–12, 112–16
Concrete labour, 23–4, 60
Conditions of work, 76
Consumption
 necessary, 9–10, 36, 46, 48, 50, 86, 87, 107
 productive, 10
 working class, 10, 36, 46, 48, 50, 86–8, 100
Control, 55, 57, 58, 67, 89–91
Conveyor-belt production, 83
Co-operation, 55–63
 development stages, 56–63
 and division of labour, 55–6, 57
 elementary, 56–7, 58
 industrial, 61–3
 manufacturing, 57–61
Corporations, multiple, 101, 102, 103
Credit cards, 18
Crisis, Keynesian, 130–1

Day, working,
 length of, 46–7, 48, 51, 82
 necessary part, 46, 48, 73
Deficit financing expansion, 128–9
Democracy, and the working class, 113–16
Depreciation, 10, 85
Developing countries, *see* Underdeveloped countries
Discipline, factory, 74
Division of labour, 55–6, 57, 58, 61–2

Economy, national
 cyclical fluctuation, 130–1
 stabilisation policies, 126–7
Employment, *see* Unemployment
Exchange, 31
 equal, 33–4, 39, 41
 money as medium, 13, 17, 20
Exchange-value, 20–1, 26
Expansion, 98–9
 deficit-financed, 128–9

Exploitation, 41–2, 44, 50, 72
 and labour intensification, 76
 and living standards, 49, 51–2
 by managerial caste, 102, 103
 underdeveloped countries, 52
 and wages, 92

Fetishism, 68, 101
Feudalism, 4–5, 9
Food, production, 94–5
Ford, Henry, 83

Gold money, 16

Hours of work, 46–7, 48, 51, 82

Immiseration of labour, 72–8
Incomes policy, 69–70, 76
Income-yielding assets, 1
Individual labour, 24–5
Industrial capital, circuit, 32–4
Industrial co-operation, 61–3
Industrial revolution, 62
Industry, global redistribution, 53
Instruments of production, 7–8
 as capital, 9
 as products, 7–8
Intensification of labour, 74–8, 83
Irrationality of capital, ix, 6, 54, 77–8, 132

Job creation, 128–30; *see also* Unemployment

Keynes, J. M., 128
Keynesian theory, 120
 crisis, 130–1
 double crisis, 130–1
 unemployment, 124–30

Labour, abstract or social, 15, 23–4, 26, 31, 60
 circuit, 30
 concrete or individual, 23–4, 60
 dead, 8, 9, 14–15
 division of, 55–6, 57, 58, 61–2
 duration of, 46–7, 48, 51, 73, 82
 general, 60
 immiseration of, 72–8

Labour *(contd)*
  individual, 24–5
  intensity of, 74–8, 83
  living, 7–8, 9, 14–15
  measurement of, 15, 21
  productive, 4–5, 132–4
  redeployment of, 15, 22–3, 65
  reserve army, 120, 124, 125
  skilled, 65–6
  underdeveloped countries, 125
  unproductive, 4–5, 129–30
  value of, 69, 70–1, 73, 76–7, 92, 126
  and labour-power, 36–8, 68–72, 73, 92
Labour-power, 34–9
  commodities needed for, 36, 37–8, 85–6, 94
  delayed payment for, 71–2
  exploitation, 41–2, 44, 49, 50, 72, 76, 102, 103
  sale of, 2, 30, 35, 40, 57, 71–2
  use-value, 36, 71
  value of, 36–8, 85, 90, 92
    reduction of, 49, 55
    and unemployment, 121–4
    and wages, 40, 68–72, 73, 85–9, 126
Labour-time
  necessary, 46, 48, 73
  surplus, 46
Living standards, rise, 5–6, 78, 85

Machinery, 8, 63–7, 74, 83, 96–7
  abolition of, 67
Managerial caste, 101–4
Manufacturing co-operation, 57–61
Marx, Karl, ix-x
Mass production, 83, 84
Material production, 7–10, 58
Means of production, 2, 38, 95
Money, 10–20
  and commodities, relation between, 13–17, 26
  definition of, 11–12, 13, 19
  as exchange medium, 13, 17, 20
  labour-time, equivalent of, 19, 26
  material form, 11, 12, 16, 17–18, 19
  value-form, 26
Monopolies, 111, 113

Ouput; *see also* Productivity
  measurement of, 59
  value of, 74

Payment for labour, delayed, 71–2
Pin-making
  labour, division of, 56, 57, 58–9, 61–2
Poverty, absolute, 1, 2, 3, 4, 6, 57–8
Price, 13, 14
  and value, 21, 34, 108
Production
  absolute limit of, 118–19
  capitalist, 25, 57–8, 60–1, 62
  centralisation of, 56–7
  collective, 57, 59–60
  control of, 55, 57, 58, 64
  cost-price of, 96, 109
  definition of, 7, 8–9, 54
  individual, 56, 59
  instruments of, 7–8, 9
  machinery in, 8, 63–7, 74, 83, 96–7
  means of, 2, 38, 95
  methods of, 49, 51, 61, 66–7, 98–9, 105
  new, 44
  organisation of, 55, 56–7, 61–2, 84
  standardisation, 66
  surplus, 10, 37–8
Productivity, 5–6
  increased, 48–9, 50, 57, 72–3
  and intensification, 74–5
  techniques, new, 49, 51, 61, 66–7, 98–9, 105
Products, 7
Profit, 31, 38–9, 92–119
  rate of, 44–5, 92–3, 116–17
    average, 105–9
    falling tendency, law, 116–18, 119, 124
  and wages, 39–40, 69
Proletarianisation of managerial caste, 103–4
Public employees, 129–30

Rational system, capital as, ix, 6, 54, 77–8, 132
Redeployment, 15, 22–3, 65
Redundancy, and machines, 67

Index

Reproduction, circuit, 10
Reserve army of labour, 120, 124, 125

Savings, working class, 2
Shift working, 82
Simple commodity production, 25
Skill, artisan, 65–6
Smith, Adam, 100
  pin-making, 56, 57, 58–9, 61–2
Social capital, 31, 39, 104–12
  organic composition, 116–19
Social class, *see* Class
Social labour, 24–5, 26
Social security benefit, 3–4
Stabilisation policies, 126–7
Standardisation, 66
Surplus production, 10, 37–8
Surplus value, 28, 31–4
  absolute, 44, 45–8, 50
  as capital, 29, 30
  maximum, 40–1, 55
  and profits, 38–9, 92
  rate of, 44, 48, 73, 78, 79–82, 93, 106
  real, 78, 82
  relative, 48–50
  combined with absolute, 51–3
  and wages, 39–40

Technical developments, 95–6
Third World, *see* Underdeveloped countries
Time
  capitalist, 83–4
  importance of, 78–85
  natural, 83–5
Tools, 8
Trade unions, 113
Transformation problem, 104–6
Transport, time, 83

Underdeveloped countries
  exploitation, 52–3
  industrialisation, 52–3, 131
  Keynesian theory, 120, 125
Unemployment, 2–3
  and accumulation, 121–4, 126, 127
  causes of, 127
  and employment of capital, 127–8
  and job creation, 128–31

Keynesian theory, 124–30
  policies, 128–31
  social security benefit, 3–4
  unavoidable, 124
Use-value, 20, 22, 26, 28, 35, 54

Value, 20–6, 109–10
  and price, 21, 34, 108
  surplus, *see* Surplus value
Variable capital, 42, 44, 50, 93, 121

Wage-form, 68–72, 77, 126, 127
Wage-goods, 49–50, 51, 66, 72, 94
Wage-labour, 58
Wages, 58, 68–91
  and capital circulation, 86–8
  compared with social security, 4
  delayed payment, 71–2
  dependence on, 3, 4
  and exploitation, 92
  and intensified labour, 75–6
  and necessary consumption, 36, 85–6
  and profits, 39–40, 69
  public employees, 129–30
  rate of, 69–70
  real, 68, 84–5
  rise in, 40, 41, 49, 70, 76, 78, 84–5, 87, 69
  struggle, 89–91
  as value of labour-power, 40, 41, 68–72, 85–9
Wealth, inequality, 1, 44, 58
Work, conditions of, 76
  necessity of, 4–5, 35–6, 96
Working class
  absolute poverty, 2, 3, 6, 58
  affluence, 2, 3, 49, 66, 78, 85
  as consumers, 10, 36, 46, 48, 50, 86–8, 100
  control of, 55, 57, 58, 64, 67
  disappearance of, 103–4
  exploitation of, 41–2, 44, 50, 72
  individual workers, 60–1, 67
  labour-power, ownership of, 2, 30, 35, 40, 57, 71–2
  and machines, 64–5, 67
  need for, 35–6

Working class (*contd*)
  poverty, 2
  reproduction of, 35–6
  savings, 2
  wages, dependence on, 2–3
Working day, length of, 46–7, 48, 51, 82
  necessary part, 46, 48, 73